Justification

Justification

Pauline Texts Interpreted in the Light of the
Old and New Testaments

by

MARKUS BARTH

translated by A. M. Woodruff III

Wipf & Stock
PUBLISHERS
Eugene, Oregon

Translated from the German *Rechtfertigung* (*Theologische Studien* 90), copyright 1969 by the EVZ Verlag, Zurich, Switzerland. The same study has appeared in the *Analecta Biblica* (1970) of the Pontifical Biblical Institute, Rome.

Wipf and Stock Publishers
199 W 8th Ave, Suite 3
Eugene, OR 97401

Justification
By Barth, Markus
Copyright©1971 by Barth, Markus
ISBN: 1-59752-850-1
Publication date 8/1/2006
Previously published by William B. Eerdmans Publishing Co., 1971

Contents

A Note on the Literature

In addition to dictionary and wordbook articles on justice, righteousness, judgment, justification, and the like, the following literature has proved to be especially important for this study:

Barth, Karl. "Church and State," in *Community, State, and Church: Three Essays* (pp. 101-49). New York: Doubleday (Anchor), 1960.

———. *Church Dogmatics* (Vol. IV, Part I, paragraph 61). Edinburgh: T. & T. Clark, 1956.

Bligh, J. *Galatians* (esp. pp. 197-224). London: St. Paul Publications, 1969.

Bornkamm, G. "Die Frage nach der Gerechtigkeit Gottes," in *Das Ende des Gesetzes* (pp. 196ff.). Munich: Chr. Kaiser Verlag, 1952.

Braun, H. *Gerichtsgedanke und Rechtfertigung bei Paulus.* Leipzig: J. C. Hinrichs, 1930.

Bultmann, Rudolf. *Theology of the New Testament* (Vol. II, pp. 270ff.). New York: Scribners, 1955.

———. "Zur Auslegung von Gal. 2, 15-18," in *Ecclesia semper reformanda* (special issue of *Evangelische Theologie* for E. Wolf, 1952, pp. 41ff.).

———. "Dikaiosyne Theou," *Journal of Biblical Literature*, LXXXIII (1964), 12ff.

Cambier, J. *L'évangile de Dieu selon l'épître aux Romains*, Vol. I (*Studia Neotestamentica* 3). Louvain: Desclée de Brouwer, 1967.

Dantine, W. *Die Gerechtmachung des Gottlosen.* Munich: Chr. Kaiser Verlag, 1959.

――――. "Die Rechtfertigungslehre als Aufgabe der gegenwärtigen systematischen Arbeit," *Evangelische Theologie*, XXIII (1963), 245ff.

Descamps, A. *Les Justes et la justice* (pp. 273ff.). Gembloux: Editions J. Duculot, S.A., 1950.

Dodd, C. H. *The Bible and the Greeks* (2d ed., pp. 42ff.). London: Hodder and Stoughton, 1935.

Iwand, H. *Rechtfertigungslehre und Christusglaube* (3d ed.; *Theologische Bücherei* 14). Munich: Chr. Kaiser Verlag, 1966.

Jepsen, A. "*Zdq* und *Zdqh* im Alten Testament," in *Gottes Wort und Gottes Land* (Festschrift for H. W. Hertzberg, ed. H. Reventlow), pp. 367ff. Göttingen: Vandenhoeck und Ruprecht, 1965.

Jeremias, J. *The Central Message of the New Testament* (pp. 51-70). New York: Scribners, 1965.

Johnson, S. "Paul and IQS," *Harvard Theological Review*, CXVIII (1955), 157ff.

Käsemann, E. "God's Righteousness in Paul," in *The Bultmann School of Biblical Interpretation: New Directions?* (Vol. 1 of *Journal for Theology and the Church*, pp. 100ff.). New York: Harper, 1965.

Kertelge, K. *Rechtfertigung bei Paulus.* Münster: Aschendorff, 1967.

Koch, K. *SDQ im AT.* Dissertation for the University of Heidelberg, 1953.

Küng, Hans. *Justification.* New York: Nelson, 1964.

Lyonnet, S. "Justification, Judgement, Redemption," in *Littérature et théologie pauliniennes* (pp. 166ff.). Louvain: Desclée de Brouwer, 1960.

Müller, C. *Gottes Gerechtigkeit und Gottes Volk.* Göttingen: Vandenhoeck und Ruprecht, 1964.

von Rad, G. *Theology of the Old Testament* (Vol. I, pp. 370ff., 383ff.). New York: Harper, 1962.

Rupp, G. *The Righteousness of God.* New York: Philosophical Library, 1953.

Schulz, S. "Zur Rechtfertigung aus Gnaden in Qumran und bei Paulus," *Zeitschrift für Theologie und Kirche*, LVI (1959), 155ff.

Schmid, H. H. *Gerechtigkeit als Weltordnung.* Tübingen: J. C. B. Mohr, 1968.

Snaith, N. H. *The Distinctive Ideas of the Old Testament* (pp. 161ff.). London: Epworth, 1953.

Stuhlmacher, P. *Gerechtigkeit Gottes bei Paulus.* Göttingen: Vandenhoeck und Ruprecht, 1965.

Introduction:

A Threefold Experiment

The Basel historian Franz Overbeck was convinced that no modern man could understand Paul, let alone agree with him. If a man presumed to understand, this was evidence to Overbeck that he did not. No one, not even a professor, is excused from this harsh judgment; nevertheless, this monograph will present an experiment in Pauline exegesis that attempts to come to some sort of understanding. Three things are tried out in this experiment: (1) a one-sided thesis, (2) a method of investigation that is generally neglected today, and (3) a not-very-customary way of presenting what Paul has to teach.

1. Justification as a juridical act

Theme and thesis: The justification of which Paul speaks in Galatians, Romans, and Philippians is to be understood as a juridical process. In speaking of justification, Paul may have consciously used concepts and images that suggest a juridical decision, its pre-conditions, its execution, and its consequences. It is generally agreed that all the Pauline assertions about righteousness, justification, gospel, faith, salvation, and life hang together. Why not, for once, present them as hanging together by virtue of their roles in a single juridical event?

Reformation and post-Reformation theology, indeed, had a great deal to say about the "forensic" character of justification. The word "forensic," however, was used only in a restricted sense to indicate that God's righteousness was fully credited to man's account and to exclude the notion of an inherent or infused righteousness deserving of God's acknowledgment. The Reformers and their successors made a distinction between *declaring* that a man is righteous and *making* him righteous. They intended to rule out every possible claim that justification either preceded or followed human merit. Justification meant that a man was looked upon by God and treated by him "as if" he himself had fulfilled what the obedient Son of God, Jesus Christ, had done. Thus that act of God counted as "forensic" in which God simply gave righteousness to the evildoer by declaration, in spite of man's being dead in sin. In the *International Critical Commentary* this "justification" is called a legal fiction.[1]

This criticism of Paul or of his interpreters might hold up on the assumption that what God does in judging and pronouncing follows a course analogous to that of human justice and is bound to the same criteria. The Reformers, however, did not wish to claim that justification corresponds to earthly juridical practice or that it could be a model for it. Theologians like Luther distinguished "divine righteousness" so sharply from earthly justice that the two could not meet in either the historical or the ethical realm—and certainly not in the juridical. A number of recent interpreters—especially C. H. Dodd in his commentary on Romans, but also S. Lyonnet, J. Jeremias, and J. Cambier (see the note on the literature)—have taken the position that justifying and judging are different things in Paul. On this view, justification is an act of fatherly mercy and creative salvation that has nothing to do with judgment and therefore cannot properly be characterized by terms from the juridical sphere.

The gracious and saving character of God's righteousness and of the miracle of the justification of the sinner cannot possibly be questioned in the following. However, with all due respect for the intention and arguments of the modern interpreters we have named, we will attempt to show that Paul's theology "is essentially theodicy," as M. Dibelius states.[2] Why else should the Apostle, trained

1 The formula "as if" appears, for example, in the Heidelberg Catechism, Q. 60. W. Sanday and A. C. Headlam may have such a formulation in mind when they speak of a "fiction"; *Romans, International Critical Commentary* (New York: Scribners, 1902), p. 367.

2 M. Dibelius and W. G. Kümmel, *Paul* (New York: Longmans, Green, 1953), pp. 63-66; M. Dibelius, "Glaube und Mystik bei Paulus," in *Botschaft und Geschichte* (Tübingen: J. C. B. Mohr, 1956), II, 94ff., esp. 106-111; "Paulus und die Mystik," *loc. cit.*, pp. 134ff., esp. p. 140.

as a rabbi and a jurist, use the concepts of righteousness (=justice) and justification, when these terms evoke unmistakable juridical associations in Old Testament, rabbinic, apocalyptic, and even modern thought? If Paul had *not* intended to talk about a juridical dispensing of divine justice, he might have chosen a terminology that simply expressed fatherly omnipotence and love. In any case, we shall assemble his assertions about God's righteousness, judgment, and justification and present the implications of these. Our synoptic view of the pertinent utterances of Paul and other biblical authors will speak for or against itself.

The material we shall survey is limited; not all of Paul's theology deals with justification or is subsidiary to it. The Apostle's doctrine of justification is variously judged to be the center of his preaching, one of many equally important parts of it, a lesser crater in the central crater of salvation, or no more than an incidental doctrine called into being by the historical necessity to polemize against a certain (supposedly Jewish) heresy.

It is certain, though, that justification and its attendant vocabulary, images, and comparisons occupy a prominent place in Paul's teaching. Alongside it are the doctrines of reconciliation, adoption, sanctification, and Christ's body, not to mention the so-called mystical features of Paul's thinking and teaching. Alongside juridical metaphors the Apostle uses imagery from the political, cultic, social, familial, biological, technological, and athletic realms. Paul's theology can be interpreted from the viewpoint of the liberation from Egypt (or the ransoming of slaves), of the Messiah's enthronement and victory over his enemies, of the uniting of Jews and Gentiles and the reconciliation with God, of adoption and house rules, of incarnation and the formation of a body, of building and edifying, of planting and growth, of following in the master's footsteps, of running a course in the arena, or of waging a war. The gospel of justification is but one of many formulations that Paul gives to the message of Christ.

In Romans 1:16-17, Paul declares that this message of Christ is his one and only concern. This essay will look at its formulation only in the gospel of justification. Even if justification is only one element among others in Paul's theology, it is certainly not the least important of the numerous strikingly original features that his writings present.

2. The Old Testament as a methodological key

Method: The determining of a method is just as limiting as the determining of a theme and the formulation of a thesis. A method can be judged appropriate only on the basis of the usefulness of the actual results that are achieved by its employment.

Since the end of the nineteenth century, it has been common practice among critical New Testament scholars to employ as keys to Paul's theology the piety of the mystery cults, mysticism, the Stoa, Gnosticism, and Jewish theology of a rabbinic, apocalyptic, or sectarian stamp. More recently, the limits of an approach to Paul from the study of the history of religions have been recognized and other methods, derived from form-critical, cult-historical, and tradition-historical inquiries, have been applied. The greatest respect should go to those interpreters who refuse to put all their eggs in one basket. In spite of the dazzling spotlight that this or that "parallel" or "tradition" may throw on an individual Pauline passage, the combined effect of diverse influences on the Apostle cannot be denied. Caution is necessary lest one-sided images of Paul be constructed.

Few scholars, however, have groped toward an explanation of Paul based on the key that his epistles themselves offer most insistently: the Old Testament. While it is *possible and probable* that Paul was acquainted with mystery religions, Qumran, Jewish apocalypticism, early forms of Jewish-Gentile Gnosticism, and the like; while it *appears to be proved* that he adopted much from the thinking, confession, and practice of Jewish and Gentile Christian congregations, it is *certain* that he referred to the Old Testament in order to make himself intelligible.

The Old Testament canon and text that Paul used were somewhat different from the printed editions of the Greek and Hebrew Old Testaments available today. Nevertheless, Paul's canon and text are close enough to our Bibles to make possible a careful checking of the quotations and allusions in the Pauline epistles. It is not just occasionally (for example, in polemical and ethical connections), but especially in developing the doctrine of justification that Paul refers with emphasis to the Old Testament as a whole or makes use of specific Old Testament passages.[3] Certain key concepts ("justify," "righteousness" or "justice," "judgment," the position of Jews and Gentiles before God's judgment) are not Paul's free inventions, but are at least partly determined by indications, intimations, and hopes that come to expression in Old Testament writings.

Since great contributions have been made toward a better understanding of the Old Testament in the last few decades, New Testament exegesis can no longer allow itself to be influenced exclusively by the Hellenistic environment of Paul. Even the tension between Christian tradition and interpretation in Paul's letters is not by itself sufficient as a hermeneutical key to Paul, for the tradition that Paul took up, opposed, furthered, or renewed had a content determined to a large extent by the Old Testament. Elements and structures of this content, in preference to its tradition-history, will now be investigated.

Five examples can show the kind of influence the Old Testament had on Paul and on the tradition he took up and reformulated.

1. The Greek verb "justify" (*dikaioō*) appears more frequently in the Septuagint than the *piel* or *hiphil* of the corresponding Hebrew word (*zdq*). The meanings "make righteous" and "declare righteous" are both inherent in it, but, as will be shown below, they do not exhaust the scope of the word. It is probable that in using this verb the Hebrew writers often thought of an orderly juridical procedure, in which justice and righteousness (and not a legal fiction!) won the day. In all probability the Greek translators of the Old Testament always thought of such a procedure. Under no circumstances did "justify" mean that black was called white. For a judge to set a

---

[3] In several instances (e.g., Rom. 1:2; 3:12) Paul avers that the doctrine he preaches is biblical. Prominent among the Old Testament texts quoted in order to illustrate the doctrine of justification are Gen. 15:6; Is. 28:16; Hab. 2:4; and Ps. 143:2. "Abraham believed the Lord, and it was reckoned to him as righteousness." "I am establishing a stone in Zion. . . . He who believes in him will not be put to shame" (so the Greek version, not the Hebrew text of Is.). "The righteous man will live by faith" (this is Paul's way of quoting Habakkuk. The text of our Hebrew Bible has "by his faithfulness"; cf. 1 Sam. 26:23; Ezek. 18:9; the Greek [LXX] translation offers the version: "by *my* faithfulness"). "No man living is righteous before you." On the altered version of Ps. 143:2, see below, note 16, p. 30.

guilty man free was just as contrary to justice—the justice that God practiced and human judges knew—as the condemnation of a guiltless man. "I will [LXX, You shall] not acquit [or, justify] the wicked" (Exod. 23:7).[4] In passages where the Hebrew author of a passage thought of a juridical proceeding only incidentally or not at all, the "Seventy," the Greek translators of the Old Testament, distinctly alluded to a courtroom situation: "Enter not into judgment with Thy servant; for no man living *is righteous* before Thee" (Hebrew Ps. 143:2); ". . . for no man living *will be justified* [or, acquitted] before Thee" (LXX Ps. 142:2).[5]

2. Paul's understanding and use of the term "righteousness of God" cannot be explained on the basis of Solon's, Aristotle's, or the Stoics' concept of (legal or moral) righteousness, but the Old Testament illustrates the Pauline meaning of this term.

(a) God's righteousness is equated, especially in Isaiah and the Psalms, with his saving intervention in the lives of individuals, of his people, and of the nations. This makes righteousness identical with saving deed, or briefly, with salvation.

(b) In other passages righteousness stands parallel to love, truth, and faithfulness. There righteousness is the right way and means of keeping the covenant between God and his chosen people. It means God's loyalty, then, but it also means a man's right attitude toward

[4] For passages with parallel contents, cf. Num. 14:18; Deut. 25:1; Mic. 6:11; Is. 5:23; 1 Kings 8:32; Susanna 53. Absalom, who did the opposite and vindicated all comers (2 Sam. 15:1ff.), serves as a bad example of a royal judge.

[5] See esp. E. W. Burton, *Galatians, International Critical Commentary*, pp. 463ff., and N. H. Watson, "Some Observations on the Use of *dikaioo* in the LXX," *Journal of Biblical Literature*, LXXIX (1960), 255ff. Watson points out that the LXX translators, even when they rendered something other than the *piel* or *hiphil* of *zdq* with *dikaioō* (e.g., Is. 1:17; Mic. 6:11; 7:9; Ezek. 21:13—in the Hebrew text 21:18), "had the picture of a judge clearly before their eyes." The same thing will hold true for Paul, for in 1 Cor. 4:3-4 and Rom. 2:12-13 the verbs "judge" and "justify" are used as parallel terms, which makes it probable that they are intended as synonyms, although the verb "judge" may have more the sense of condemning and "justify" more the sense of acquitting. It will be shown below that the acquittal that results from justification does not exclude prior condemnation but comes *through* it. Cf. the joining of "sin, righteousness and judgment" in John 16:8-11. For John the Evangelist's doctrine of justification, see Th. Preiss, "Justification in Johannine Thought," in *Life in Christ* (tr. H. Knight; *Studies in Biblical Theology* 13, 1954), pp. 7ff.

God *and* toward his covenant partners. No tension is found between God's free intervention in history and his consistent behavior according to the promises and stipulations of the covenant. In both cases the concept of righteousness does not indicate a norm that is superior to God, but rather God's free will and his truthfulness.

(c) Indeed, as H. H. Schmid (see the note on the literature) has demonstrated, the Hebrew word for "righteousness" points to cosmic order. To "judge," accordingly, means to acknowledge this order and to restore it. In the Bible, however, God, the creator of all things and gracious Lord of all, is this valid, righteous order in person. This order includes and guarantees the salvation that is created and attested in Israel's election and history; it also includes the communal bond that has been represented for some time in the scholarly literature as the essence of the biblical concept of righteousness.

(d) The manifestation of God's righteousness is bound up with the showing and exercising of his power. It aims at reciprocity: man is to show such righteousness and truthfulness as correspond to God's. For this reason right and might—that is, saving action, enforcement of justice, and recognition of God's law and righteousness—are inextricably bound up together. The power of God's righteousness is exemplified by the fact that "he kills and brings to life, forces into the pit and brings back out." "I kill and I make alive; I wound and heal." "I bring low the high tree, and make high the low tree, I dry up the green tree, and make the dry tree flourish."[6] The boon of God's righteousness is the life of men. God is not praised by the dead.

3. The relative position before God of Jews and Gentiles is definitely an Old Testament theme.

(a) Popular oracles collected in the prophetic books and many royal Psalms contain the promise that God, either directly or through the judges and kings established by him, would condemn and annihilate the peoples inimical to himself and his people. "You shall dash them in pieces like a potter's vessel." "He will shatter kings on the day of his wrath. He will execute judgment among the nations, filling them with corpses."[7] Balaam the Moabite was

[6] 1 Sam. 2:6; Deut. 32:39; Ezek. 17:24. Cf. the lamentation and thanksgiving Psalms, e.g., Ps. 22 and 88.

[7] Ps. 2:9; 110:5f.; cf. 68:1, etc.

17

charged by his king to assure the victory of the Moabites over Israel with prophetic words, but his imprecation was turned into a blessing. 1 Kings 22 shows that Israel's prophets were expected to perform a corresponding service for the salvation of Israel at the expense of the Gentiles. In the proclamation or recitation of "oracles against the nations," they probably even did it.

(b) But Amos signalled a change. The voice of the thunder of judgment that Amos received from Zion and had to transmit applied not only to Damascus, Gaza, and Tyre but with equal force to Judah and Israel. Isaiah, Jeremiah, and other prophets had to pronounce judgment more sharply against their own people than against the Gentiles. It began to look as if predictions of salvation and peace that pertained only to Israel or Judah were about to vanish. Jeremiah pilloried the cheap prophets of peace. The second Isaiah joined announcements of salvation for Israel with similar announcements for the nations and the islands. When Jonah finally let himself be constrained to announce the fall of the Gentile city Nineveh, it was he who had to learn how great is God's clemency for Gentiles who repent.

Thus the Old Testament itself knows a history of judgment imagery in which annihilation and establishment, curse and blessing follow each other far and near, somehow mysteriously bound together.

4. In the prophets and the Psalms we encounter the idea of a great and final litigation (*ribh*) between God and his people or between God and the world.[8] In late prophetic and apocalyptic writings this idea becomes more and more solid. The great judgment is pushed from the middle of time out to the boundary of the present world and time. It becomes the Last Judgment, which is marked by the resurrection of all or many of the dead and consti-

---

[8] Ps. 82; Is. 3:13-17; Mic. 6:1-8; Jer. 2:4-13; Is. 41:21-29; 43:12, etc. Cf. H. Gunkel and J. Begrich, *Einleitung in die Psalmen* (Göttingen: Vandenhoeck und Ruprecht, 1933), pp. 75, 365ff.; F. M. Cross, "The Council of Yahweh in Second Isaiah," *Journal of Near Eastern Studies*, XII (1953), 274ff.; H. B. Huffmann, "The Covenant Lawsuit in the Prophets," *Journal of Biblical Literature*, LXXVIII (1959), 285ff.; H. Boeker, "Anklage- und Verteidigungsreden im AT," *Evangelische Theologie*, XX (1960), 398ff.; C. Müller, *Gottes Gerechtigkeit und Gottes Volk* (Göttingen: Vandenhoeck und Ruprecht, 1964), pp. 57-72.

tutes the beginning of a new heaven and a new earth. Those who are faithful trust with certainty that God will prove his righteousness and that with his righteousness he will also establish the righteousness of his elect—indeed, that all creation will be renewed and made glorious.

5. This divine litigation corresponds in manner to the procedure that has been divinely prescribed and is followed on earth by the courts of Israel.[9] In Israel there could be only one kind of justice. This principle holds not only for the equal position of Israelites and sojourners before the law but also for the relation of divine justice to the justice practiced on earth. God's own justice is entrusted to the earthly king. "O God, give your justice to the king and your righteousness to the king's son."[10] Since a distinction between divine and earthly justice is unthinkable, every court is held in the name of God.

The judge is addressed as the helper or redeemer of the party that considers itself wronged. The mere fact that a case is taken up by a court in session (in the gate, in the royal palace or in the sanctuary) can be called justification or righting the wrong (Heb., *ziddeq* or *hizdiq*; Greek, *dikaioō*). God himself is implored in Psalm 43 for the boon of a hearing. During the proceedings "witnesses" take the place of advocates. Also, plaintiffs and defendants, together with the friends and relatives who support them, are considered witnesses in every way. The juridical conflict, carried on with considerable raising of voices and dramatic gestures, is like a fight between the two parties and ends with the "victory" of that party which the judge pronounces right.

The judge's duty is not only to listen carefully to the witnesses and to pronounce wisely and justly, but also to execute the judg-

---

[9] Examples of human juridical proceedings are described in 1 Sam. 22:6-19; Jer. 26; 1 Kings 3 and 21. The New Testament statements about the trial of Jesus (Mark 14–15 and parallels) and the reconstruction of the juridical order in the rabbinic tractate *Sanhedrin* are too late and too contradictory to give a picture of the procedure that was current at the time of the prophets. For a description of the juridical practices followed in Israel, see J. Pedersen, *Israel, Its Life and Culture* (London: Oxford University Press, 1954), pp. 406ff.; R. de Vaux, *Ancient Israel*, tr. J. McHugh (New York: McGraw-Hill, 1961), pp. 155ff.

[10] Ps. 72:1-2; Is. 9:6; 11:4; Jer. 23:6, etc.

ment, for example, immediately carrying out the death penalty, punishing false witnesses in proportion to the amount of damage they intended to do to the opposing party, restoring stolen goods, or dispatching agents to carry out the judgment in a distant place. (In the case of Solomon's judgment the threatened execution of the judgment assisted the investigation!)

Lastly, the juridical event includes the recognition and acceptance of the judgment by the affected parties and by everyone else who hears of the judgment. The public praise of the judge was denoted in biblical times by the verb "justify." "You must be justified in your sentence and blameless in your judgment."[11] Recent terminology, following passages such as Isaiah 45:23,[12] speaks of "exhomologesis" or *Gerichtsdoxologie.*[13] The judgment that has been passed, especially when associated with a sacrifice or sanctuary, is considered to be God's judgment and the judgment itself is considered divine (in the sense of the medieval "ordeal" or "trial by fire"). For example, a man hanging on a tree was, even after the execution, "accursed by God."[14]

These examples from the realm of Old Testament juridical thinking, practices, and expectations open up the possibility that Paul has taken some of his key thoughts—if not a whole scheme of thinking—from the Old Testament. The use he makes of the verb "justify," for example, will show whether this is in fact the case. It is striking that Paul does not use one of the many meanings the word has in classical and contemporary Greek: to "consider just" or "demand as one's

[11] Ps. 51:4; cf. Rom. 3:4; Luke 7:29, 35. Examples of such praise of a judge's righteousness are the awe before the king and the homage to the Queen of Sheba (1 Kings 3:28; 10:1-10). God's righteousness is praised in Is. 41:26; Ps. 7:11; 9:8; 11:7; 19:9; 96:10; 119:137; 145:17; Rev. 16:5, 7; 19:2, with the words, "He is right. . . . God is a righteous judge. . . . He judges the world with righteousness. . . . The Lord is just in all his ways and kind in all his doings. . . . Righteous art Thou. . . . The judgments of the Lord are true and righteous."

[12] Cf. Rom. 14:11; Phil. 2:10-11. Passages like Is. 55:12; Ps. 103:20-22, and the Song of the 3 Young Men 35ff. show that it is not only human knees that bend before the Lord and Judge. Mountains and hills fall down before him; the trees clap their hands, and good and evil powers, angels, demons, and all of God's creatures join in the doxology.

[13] G. von Rad, *Theology of the Old Testament, passim.*

[14] Deut. 21:22-23; cf. Gal. 3:13.

right." The verb, like its Hebrew equivalents, has at least three meanings in Paul, all of them reminiscent of Old Testament precedents: (1) to grant the boon of an orderly juridical procedure; (2) to bring down a righteous judgment, which consists in condemning the guilty, in pronouncing the innocent free, *and* in the corresponding public treatment of both; and (3) to praise the wise and just judge. Paul's references to Old Testament juridical thought and practice extend also to the choice of other words. Often they have the form of explicit quotations and implicit allusions.

All of the Old Testament elements we have mentioned are presupposed in our attempt to explore, sort out, and, if possible, illuminate what Paul has to say about justification.

3. Narration with wonder and admiration

Exposition: The form chosen for the body of this study is meant to correspond to the goal and route of the experiment. Instead of a systematic treatment of justification, an "admirer's narration"[15] of the miracle of justification will be given. The more conventional sort of "scholarly" argument will appear only in the footnotes. The action of justification itself calls for a substantive report that enumerates in sequence the ongoing events and changing situations. The footnotes can take no more than a subordinate role. The more dramatic the forensic action, the more the trial itself and the account of it will come to resemble a drama. It is not for nothing that the Gospels and the Book of Revelation, the liturgies of the Eastern Church and the passion plays of the Western Church, and the works of a writer like Dorothy Sayers have given dramatic expression to the dramatic Christ-event.

Who can say what is unspeakable, and who can describe what no eye has seen? Yet as a priestly writer praised the Creator by choosing a seven-day structure for describing the miraculous order of God's miraculous work, so in the following, five days in the process of justification will be distinguished. Within each day are several scenes or peculiar confrontations.

---

15 The German term *rühmende Nacherzählung* was apparently coined by G. von Rad; cf., e.g., *Theology of the Old Testament,* I, 111.

Five Aspects of God's Judgment

The First Day:

The Last Judgment Is at Hand

1. There is but one judge, God

For a long time and with almost inconceivable patience God has kept to himself in the face of the ravings of the godless; now he finally rises up in flaming anger. He summons all Jews and Gentiles to assemble before his throne, in order to expose "all ungodliness and unrighteousness of men who suppress the truth by unrighteousness" and to see to it that they harvest what they have sown. He now proves himself to be "judge over the world."[1] The moan, "How long, O Lord, how long . . . ?" and the desperate or furious cry for the appearance of the God of vengeance are stilled. At last God is waiting no longer, but has decided to exercise his royal prerogative.[2] Earlier acts of judgment concerned individual men, Israel, or at most some of the nations; this time God is judging the whole earth and every man together. While there are many judges handling the law and using power within the jurisdictions entrusted to them, God is now judging the universe, including the judges, petty and supreme. He has jealously kept the final judgment for himself. No one can cope with all the unrighteousness and injustice of the world and master it except God. Therefore, it is good that God rises up for judgment.

Those who have heard of God and have had to transmit what they have heard can in no way get around God's vehement anger against evil. God's anger is the temperature of his love. Only God's own vehemence against all sin is able to check injustice on earth.

[1] Rom. 1:18–3:20; esp. 1:18; 3:6.
[2] Ps. 4; 82; 93–94; 96–99; Is. 52:7ff.; Hab. 2:1-20, etc.

25

The judgment now beginning is the eschatological judgment. It is hardly mentioned in the priestly writings, mentioned more in the prophets, and, finally, described in lurid colors by the apocalypticists. Although it has not been spoken of for a long time, although many did not give it much mind, although others thought of its approach only with fear and trembling, now it is taking place. The court session, its procedure, and decision are publicly announced even in the capital city of the world, Rome.[3]

One can give learned and unlearned names to the fulfilment of that which has been predicted and seen in visions. One man speaks of "demythologizing" because everything that is described by mythical intimations at other times—before and afterward—at this time takes on the crass and naked form of definite events and unambiguous meaning. Another man would rather speak of "realized eschatology" or the "presence of eternity," because there is more at hand than a change in speech and signification: here occurs the complete self-manifestation of the Creator in the realm of creation, of the Holy One among the sinners, of the Lord among his servants and enemies, of the Eternal in space and time. Still another man prefers to call it the "meaning of all history," the "crisis of all crises," the "principle of hope," the "end of all religiosity," or something of the kind. Whatever name, label or interpretation this event is given, the day of God's judgment is not just any day but the "day of the Lord" or the "day of salvation," and it is breaking *today, now*.[4] What was to come, is come. That is effected and effective which was, according to the word given by God, clearly in process for a long time and was, in the light of the human revolt against God and the ensuing misery, long overdue. No Supreme Court of the future will have superior jurisdiction or be able to question what takes place now and today in this court.

3 Rom. 1:16-17. The Apostle's own judgment of the world would not be of any special interest. It was known well enough how Jews and Gentiles judged each other: mutual contempt prevailed over moderate opinions and obscured from view the fact that they did borrow from each other. Paul would have had reason to be ashamed to repeat these judgments, and they would hardly have been worth a trip to Rome. But this journey was necessary and was planned because Paul had to announce *God's* judgment. He had good reason to be "not ashamed" of that court and verdict of which, by divine commission, he was messenger among the nations.

4 Amos 5:18; Is. 2:12; Zeph. 1:14-15; 2 Cor. 6:2; Rom. 1:18; 3:21.

2. The Gentiles are convicted

The day of the Lord catches the nations red-handed. God's anger strikes men precisely where they believed they were closest to divinity: their religion. Absolutely everything that they considered cultic, holy, and wise is exposed as ingratitude, stupidity, obscurantism, and idol-making, the confounding of God with a miserable creature.[5] The immoral and perverse turn their way of life has taken in things sexual, intellectual, and social is by far not the worst, for their abominable conduct is not the reason for God's anger but the consequence of it. In delivering the Gentiles into foul practices, God proves to their faces that the life they have chosen and praised is no life at all but a prelude to chaos, "deserving of death." This is true in spite of their recognized longing and searching for ways of behaving that are "true, honorable, just, pure, lovely, gracious, virtuous [lit., a virtue] and worthy of praise."[6]

Until now the Gentiles have *not* been measured by the law of Moses. Now they are weighed in court. Now it becomes evident that in their attitudes they are "enemies" of God and are legally "dead in trespasses."[7] Are they not then excused because of their ignorance of God's will or Moses' law? By no means! The works that God has completed since the days of creation—calling and blessing the patriarchs, freeing Israel from Egypt, conquering the promised land, chastising and pardoning individuals and the people of Israel—all these were a light that shone among the Gentiles, a light they could have heeded. Pharaoh, for example, chose to ignore God's work in the freeing of Israel; and like him all the nations reacted by harden-

---

5 Rom. 1:21-23; Eph. 4:17-19. Passages from Ephesians are quoted here and in the following along with the other Pauline texts, in spite of the disputed authenticity of the Epistle to the Ephesians. Even if the letter should have come from a disciple of Paul, it still presents an important attempt to summarize Paul's message.

6 Rom. 1:24-32; Phil. 4:8.

7 Col. 1:21; 2:13; Eph. 2:1-2. Since the law that threatens its transgressors with death was not given to the Gentiles (Rom. 2:14; 3:2; 9:4, 31; 1 Cor. 9:21), the Gentiles are not condemned by the law. "All who have sinned without the law will also perish without the law" (Rom. 2:12). Sin and death do rule even without the law, as Paul intends to demonstrate in Rom. 5:12-14 by pointing to the situation that prevailed in the temporal interval between Adam and Moses.

ing their hearts.[8] Therefore the position of the nations before God's judgment is "hopeless."[9]

3. The Jews are condemned

There is one people among the assembled nations that appears to be little affected by all this—the Jews. They are prepared for God to make himself known as Judge and to render judgment. God has certainly revealed his will to them. They "know his will" even when they do not do it. They were elected for this and are conscious of themselves as "leaders of the blind" and a "light" in the dark world. Through the privileges God has granted them—the election and blessing of Abraham, the safe conduct out of Egypt and the protection in the desert, the covenant renewed again and again, the gift of the law and the land, and continued acts of chastisement and mercy—through these deeds God has been revealing himself to them for a long time. While the Gentiles refused to honor God, the chosen people was eventually named the "Jews" after the tribe of Judah, a name that has sometimes been interpreted etymologically as meaning "I will praise the Lord."[10]

Certain of their distinction, a few Jews now make reference in God's court to the Torah scrolls handed down to them, and they speak of the mark they are proud to bear, circumcision. Law and circumcision are supposed to demonstrate bodily, historically, and existentially that these people are God's property. They have already experienced special treatment as God's "chosen people" and so they have high expectations of further preference. Thus they are willing enough to recognize God's right to condemn the Gentiles, just as Jonah the prophet once expected with certainty that God would carry out his threats. As justice takes its course against the Gentiles, the Jews will be present in a more than passive fashion. They are ready to judge and condemn the Gentiles on their own. They reason that everyone who heartily condemns sin and sinners will surely "escape the judgment of God." It is not as though they want to

[8] Rom. 1:19-20; 9:17; Eph. 4:17-19.
[9] Eph. 2:12.
[10] Rom. 2:17-29; 3:2; 9:4; Gal. 3:15-24. In Rom. 2:17ff. there is a clear allusion to Gen. 29:35.

replace God and God's judgment, but they think it appropriate that they should occupy jury seats on the right and left of the Judge.[11]

With this attempt they come to grief. The Torah and the circumcision in which they pride themselves are not admitted, either as mitigating circumstances or as "good works" in lieu of the fulfilment of the whole will of God, which is lacking.[12] As for the prophets, Amos has already said clearly enough that the coming judgment of God would fall on Judah and Israel too. Thus the law given to Israel is neither a letter of protection from juridical persecution nor a license for jury duty. Rather it serves as a reminder of God's judgment and a summons to appear before his bar. The Torah gives fair warning to those who receive it that they as well as the Gentiles have been apprehended in the ways of sin, of idol-making, of folly, and of hardening of the heart. It tells the Jews, "You break up marriages; you plunder the temple; you dishonor God by transgressing the law." By the law, accordingly, sin is not removed but is "known" and "counted" as sin, even aroused and revived.[13] In point of fact, not only the Gentiles but also the children of Israel have "confounded the glory of the imperishable God with the image and form of perishable men, or of birds, beasts, and snakes."[14] Even Israel had to be reminded by her prophets that images are foolishness.[15]

---

[11] Rom. 2:1-3; cf. Mark 10:35-40; Matt. 19:28.

[12] Circumcision is useless as a selective and isolated fulfilment of the law, according to Gal. 5:3, 6:13, and Rom. 2:25. It carries the obligation to maintain the whole law, and it has significance only when it rests on the basis of the election covenant and serves as a reminder of the circumcision of the heart of which prophetic Old Testament voices spoke (Jer. 4:4; 9:25-26; Ezek. 44:7, 9; Deut. 10:16; Lev. 26:41). Even in contemporary Jewish terminology a *mitzvah* (commandment) is an "opportunity to do God's will," not a substitute for the fulfilment of all the commandments.

[13] Rom. 2:21-24; 3:20; 4:15; 5:13; 7:9, 11, 13.

[14] E.g., in praying to the golden calf of Bethel and to the one on Sinai; also in the veneration of Nehushtan (2 Kings 18:4); cf. Rom. 1:23. The phrase "all ungodliness and unrighteousness of men" indicates that Rom. 1:18-32 cannot pertain only to the Gentiles. The Old Testament texts to which Rom. 1:23 alludes (Jer. 2:11; Deut. 4:15-19; Ps. 106:20) concern the erroneous ways of Israel and not only or primarily the idolatry of the Gentiles. (The only exception is Wisd. 12:24.)

[15] For example, Is. 40:18ff.; 46:5ff.

An Israelite who acknowledges the righteousness of God and the law does not for that reason consider himself to be faultless but knows that he stands under God's judgment. For this reason, in Old Testament times Israelites were praying: "Enter not into judgment with Thy servant, for no man living is righteous before Thee."[16] A Jew who prays thus is far from imagining that only the Gentiles are sinners.[17] In his prayer there is great emphasis on the confession, "We Jews cannot save ourselves by ourselves or escape from God's judgment." He is a true Jew who knows that the judgment begins with God's own house in Jerusalem.[18] Rather than claiming the status of a law-abiding man, he confesses that, measured against the standard of the law, he is a dead man. "When the law came, sin sprang to life. But I died. . . . Through the law I died. . . ." The law is indeed "given for life," but it does not have the power to confer life. On the contrary, "the letter kills."[19]

Since, therefore, not even a part of the chosen people can escape the righteous anger of God, it is obvious that no flesh can stand as righteous by itself. "Every mouth is stopped. The whole world is subject to the judgment of God."[20] No flesh—that means no circumcised Jewish flesh. Every mouth—that means even the mouth that

16 Ps. 143:2. When Paul quotes this passage in Gal. 2:16 and Rom. 3:20, he replaces the words "is righteous" with the LXX "will be justified." He further enriches the Psalm text with elements from Gen. 6:3 and 8:21. Or has he quoted 1 Enoch 81:5, the Qumran text 1QH IX:14f.—cf. VII:28—or a Targum?

17 Gal. 2:15 appears to prove the opposite. On philological grounds, however, this verse should not be translated "We, Jews by birth and not sinners from the Gentiles" but, as Luther intimated in his first commentary on Galatians, "We are sinners of Jewish origin and not of Gentile descent." Here, as in Rom. 3:22-23, it is made clear that Jews and Gentiles are sinners "without distinction." But it is also established that the equality of the Jews' and the Gentiles' sin does not prevent their sin from coming about in different ways. Gentiles sin "without the law," Jews "under the law"; see Rom. 2:12. In Gal. 2:15 both the equality and the difference are affirmed.

18 Jeremiah and Ezekiel said this clearly enough. Cf. Jer. 25:29; Ezek. 9:5f. According to 1 Pet. 4:17 the Christian church must apply this proposition to herself.

19 Rom. 7:9-10 in the phrasing of the New English Bible; Gal. 2:19; 3:21; 2 Cor. 3:6.

20 Rom. 3:19-20, 27; 10:3; Phil. 3:9.

murmurs the law texts and the commandments. The whole world—
that means especially the religious world.[21]

4. There are no exceptions

Once more there is whispering among the Jews and Gentiles
assembled before the court. Are there not selected Gentiles who—in
morals if not in religion—stand head and shoulders above the Jews
and are therefore able to escape the Judgment? When certain Gentiles, not obeying an externally given law but autonomously following an unwritten inner law, do what the law requires, do they not
deserve to be brought out of hiding into the light?[22] And are there
not other Gentiles who—on their own or influenced by the synagogues of the Diaspora, by Jewish missionary literature, or by
Palestinian Christian preachers—have adopted specific Jewish ordinances such as circumcision, dietary practices, and observance of the
Sabbath?[23] The latter group is now made to understand clearly that
submission to an arbitrary selection of ordinances is no substitute
for fulfilling the whole law through love. If not even the fleshly
children of Abraham—those who are given the law and commandments—are protected from sin and its consequences, how are Gentiles to be justified by a few arbitrarily selected "works of the law"?

The first group, however, is giving itself up to a fiction if they
believe that some natural law, superior to the law of Sinai or
substituted for it, can be so strong and influential in the hearts of
certain men that they possess immunity from God's judgment.
Indeed, how can the *Gentiles* do on their own that which Israel has

---

[21] The apparently generalizing statements about sin, which seem to have
been formed without attention to individual cases, are in reality aimed
specifically at and refer to chosen, pious, religious men. They do not intend to
say: "Even *they* are sinners who stand at a distance and are unknown to us,"
but rather: "Even I will be judged as a sinner. . . . Even *we* are found to be
sinners" (Rom. 3:7; Gal. 2:16-17). The Old Testament passages assembled in
Rom. 3:10-18 come from penitential prayers and cries for help. They should
not be taken as a cheap condemnation of the whole world. They do not serve
in the end as an excuse that is occasionally sought for one's own sins in the sea
of the sins of humanity.

[22] Cf. Rom. 2:14-16.

[23] The heretics whom Paul opposes in Galatians and Colossians had obviously chosen this way.

31

not brought about in spite of her ardent endeavor?[24] Individual Gentiles, if they were like the penitent and pardoned Ninevites in the Jonah story, would be able to stand before God's judgment; and so would men who have the law of God written on their hearts as Jeremiah predicted for the saved people of God in the last times.[25] But at the outset of God's judgment, there is no man in heaven or on earth, among the Jews or the Gentiles, who can *excuse himself.* "No one is righteous; no, not one; . . . All have sinned and failed to give glory to God."[26] As with the righteous Job, who "could not answer him once in a thousand times," a fearful silence sets in before the throne of the angry Judge—the silence of guilt.[27]

Dies irae, dies illa
solvet saeclum in favilla
teste David et Sybilla.

Quantus tremor est futurus,
quando judex est venturus,
cuncta stricte discussurus.

Judex ergo cum sedebit,
quidquid latet apparebit,
nil in ultrum remanebit.

Quid sum miser tunc dicturus?
Quem patronum rogaturus,
cum vix justus sit securus?[28]

---

24 Rom. 9:30-31; 10:2-3.

25 Rom. 2:14-16 is probably a parallel to Jer. 31:33-34; Is. 45; Matt. 12:41; and Gal. 2:16, and therefore no more a biblical Magna Charta for natural law than Rom. 1:19-20 is for natural theology.

26 Rom. 1:20; 2:1; 3:10-18, 23.

27 Cf. Job 9:3; Rev. 8:1.

28 "O day of wrath! On that day the age will be destroyed in ashes, as David and the Sybil have attested. O what fear there will be when the Judge comes to bring all things strictly to naught! When the Judge takes his seat, whatever has been hidden will appear and nothing will remain unavenged. What then am I, miserable man, to say? Who is to be sought as a protector when even the righteous man is hardly safe?" Cf. Zeph. 1:15.

5. Is this a Pyrrhic victory for God?

While palling silence rules—red faces here, teeth gnashing there—it is unambiguously clear that God alone is holy, living, powerful, and righteous. Before him and around him, on the other hand, lies a field of the spiritually, legally, and morally dead. They may vegetate physically and claim that they still exist, but a life that has been forfeited is not a life worth the name.

Is this God's juridical victory? Is this the end of his ways and the result of his action? Is all this justice and righteousness? If so, God's triumph would be won at the expense of men. One would have to conclude that the establishment of his dominion meant the final abasement of everything human. There would remain a God whose creative will and work of creation have not reached their goal. As Creator he would have blundered and failed. If man, who was created in God's image and likeness, is finally unmasked as a grotesque caricature, then suspicion falls on the original. Such a result would show God to have been unsuccessful even in the electing of Israel. Precisely because the setting apart of this people led to pride and self-praise—to an attitude that not only matched the foolish fantasy of the Gentiles but surpassed it in outrageousness—even the election appears discredited as pernicious.

Will God now really repudiate his revelation, his creation, his words of election, promise, and law? Will he at the end have no other word left for his creatures than the judgment *Condemned?* This would mean vindication for Marcionites, or Manichaeans, or Ophites, and perhaps all doubt-ridden men as well, all who curse or are cursed. Perhaps even suicides would be proved right. It would be God himself who had vindicated them—if the judgment and its objective were at this moment completed. Then only a masochist could rejoice in the glory of God. God's holiness would consist only in the fact that he is totally other than the sinners. His will and power to make the sinner holy would not be an essential part of it. He would be a living God in that he would live only at the expense of the men into whom he once blew the breath of life. He would be all in all by virtue of having proved that man is nothing. He would be true to himself by making triumphant a devastating concept of righteousness—at the expense of man. The bitter adage would apply even to God: *Summum jus, summa injuria.*

Is *this* God's righteousness? Is *this* to be the triumph of theodicy? Did the promise of God's final judgment mean nothing but this? And will all who waited and hoped, with fear and trembling, for this Judgment at last reap nothing else but total destruction?

The Second Day:

The Mediator Is Appointed, Acts, and Dies

1. The advocate is appointed

In the light of the situation that has arisen, there is only one who can be of any help and can save from the threatened general destruction: God himself. He does not intend to enjoy his own life at the expense of uncounted masses of miserable and dead men. He will not remain righteous himself at the price of eternal condemnation for all. He does not want to rule over a gaping emptiness. Therefore, he has decided from eternity *not* to treat the nations and his chosen people according to what they have deserved but according to the measure of what is needful for them.

The terrible predicament of the nations and of God's chosen people can be changed only by the intervention in God's court of a reliable, bold, and skillful advocate. Legal aid and assistance are required. Help cannot come from hitherto hidden evidence, from the public display of a few isolated works of compliance to the law, from the demonstration of basically fine convictions, from the utterance of true words, or from the promise of future betterment. God's righteous anger cannot be appeased by cultic apparatus, the fat of sacrifices, songs, Bible verses, vows, or even magical practices. Under the present circumstances there are no means that could mediate between God and man and build a saving bridge. But the possibility remains, judging by minor precedents found in the earlier history of God and man, that a mediator might "stand in the breach."[1] After the pattern of Abraham, Moses, the high priest, and

[1] Cf. Jer. 18:20 (but also 15:1, 11!); Ezek. 22:30; Ps. 106:23. The Old Testament shows that long before Paul's time even the best and strongest

many prophets and righteous men, he would have to stand up for those subject to damnation and "pray for the evildoers."[2]

Such an intercessor cannot be appointed by men from the ranks of either the Gentiles or Israel. If there is to be an advocate at all whom God can hear and who can free men from death and damnation, he must be a "witness in heaven," a "surety on high," that is, someone whose voice would certainly get through to God and be heeded by him.[3] On every occasion in the history of God with men that a valid representative role is attributed to a particular person, whether for the chosen people or for the many (Gentiles), this person is chosen and appointed by God. Neither kings, nor priests, nor prophets, and certainly not the miscellaneous minor official benefactors and malefactors of Israel name themselves to the dignity and burden of being a representative. Nor are they elected to this by the people (although it is fitting and proper, as Saul's election to the kingship shows, for the people to recognize God's selection afterwards with public celebration and to make it their own). In the Last Judgment no man (not even Moses as epitomizing law or Elijah as epitomizing prophecy) can be invoked for assistance by the mass of the guilty. All men, even charismatic leaders, belong to "all flesh," which cannot justify either itself or anything else. "Truly no man can ransom himself [or, his brother]."[4]

instruments of the covenant (e.g., God's appearance and promise; the gift of the law, the land, the temple; the institutions of sacrifice, priestly dynasties, holy times, and holy wars) offer no assurance by themselves that Israel will have peace and will live. There must be a true servant of God, a so-called "covenant mediator" on duty and at work—or else the holy events and things will not be significant and effective. On the concept of the covenant mediator, see M. Noth, *The Laws in the Pentateuch and Other Essays*, tr. D. R. Ap.-Thomas (London: Oliver and Boyd, 1966), pp. 114ff.; H. W. Wolf, "Yahve als Bundesmittler," *Vetus Testamentum*, VI (1956), 316ff. Cf. Heb. 8:6, 9:15, 12:24; Gal. 3:19-20; 1 Tim. 2:5.

[2] Abraham—Gen. 18:22-23; Moses—Exod. 32:11-14; 30—34; Num. 14: 13-20; Deut. 1:37; 3:26; 4:21; 9:17-20, 25-29; Ps. 106:23; the high priest— Exod. 28:15, 30, 38; Lev. 10:17; 16 *passim*; Num. 16:47-48; Samuel—1 Sam. 12:19, 23; Amos—Amos 7:2-3; Jeremiah—Jer. 15:11, etc.; Ezekiel—Ezek. 4:4-8; the king—2 Sam. 24:17; the suffering servant—Is. 53:4, 12; a righteous man—Ezra 9:6—10:1; Neh. 9:16-37.

[3] Job 16:19; 17:3; 19:25; 33:23-25. According to 1 Sam. 2:25, Eli doubted whether there could be a mediator between God and sinful man.

[4] Ps. 49:8-10.

But now God surprises the court by sending his son. "But when the time was fulfilled, God sent his son. . . . In view of the inability of the law, which was weak because of the flesh, God sent his Son in the likeness of sinful flesh."[5] Jesus Christ was sent to be an advocate (in biblical language a "witness") for the accused. "God appointed him as an intercessor,"[6] which means as a mediator, a pleader, a defense attorney, or, in the Swiss-German language, a *Fürsprech* (speaker-for-us).

The immediate result of this appointment is clear: "We have a [legal] advocate with the Father, Jesus Christ the righteous."[7] God sends a person, not a thing. The one who is sent is pre-existent, not the product of a whim. He is *mediator* in matters of reconciliation,

[5] Gal. 4:4; Rom. 8:3; cf. John 3:16; 1 John 4:9. See also E. Schweizer, "Der religionsgeschichtliche Hintergrund der Sendungsformel," *Zeitschrift für die neutestamentliche Wissenschaft*, XXXVII (1966), 199ff.

[6] Rom. 3:25. Cf. the emphasis in Heb. 5:1, 4-6, on the appointment by God himself of the High Priest and of Jesus Christ. The wording of Rom. 3:25 is probably not formulated entirely by Paul—or perhaps not formulated by him at all—but appears to be borrowed from a tradition that also shows itself in Hebrews and the First Epistle of John. The verb translated "appoint" (*protithēmi*) and the noun translated "intercessor" (*hilastērion*) call for a brief clarification.

(1) The verb can mean, among other things, (1) to plan, (2) to bring to prominence or appoint, and (3) to publish, make known. It appears in Rom. 3:25 to be used in a sense analogous to that of the Hebrew verb *nathan* ("give," but also "set, appoint"; cf. Lev. 17:10). What Paul means by "set" or "arrange" in 1 Cor. 12:18, 28, is called "giving" in Eph. 4:11 (and also in John 3:16?).

(2) The substantive *hilastērion* is, properly speaking, a substantivized form of an adjective, and could be translated "reconciling" or something similar. Following R. K. Yerkes, *Sacrifice in Greek and Roman Religion and Early Judaism* (New York: Scribners, 1952), pp. 178ff., it is probably best to translate the Greek word in such a way as to make it clear that the root meaning is "to pray out" (*exhilaskesthai*). In the Septuagint the neuter of the adjective either means the so-called "mercy seat," i.e., the cover of the ark of the covenant (cf. Heb. 9:5)—a meaning that would make little sense in Rom. 3:25—or it has the more general meaning, current in Greek, of any "means of reconciliation." Since in Rom. 3:25 "faith" and "blood" are named as such instruments, it is probable that *hilastērion* does not refer to a third means. Then what could it mean? *Hilastērion* can be the *masculine* accusative of the original adjective and then refer to the *person* of a reconciler. Material analogies, if not linguistic ones, are so numerous in the Old and New Testaments that they cannot be neglected; see note 2 above for a list of Old Testament intercessory figures.

[7] 1 John 2:1.

not a mere *medium* or means to a good end. Thus he is more than such Old Testament antitypes or prototypes as the mercy seat and the special kinds of sacrifice. If he is indeed a means or instrument, it is only as he mediates *in person* between God and man. He is the "one mediator between God and men."[8] The Last Judgment is not a matter of continuing the shadows and foreshadowings of the Old Testament cult, but rather the verification and validation of the earlier symbolic practices through the Son, whom God establishes for the benefit of Israel and all nations as their common, fully authorized, and final priest and prophet. The Anointed of God, who was promised and is now come, is to take up, carry through, and finish what has been done in various situations by an Abraham, a Moses, a prophet, or a servant of God. The "righteousness of God" that was "promised beforehand through the prophets and in the holy scriptures," "attested by the law and the prophets," is now manifested.[9]

The Son sent from God must stand entirely on the side of those accused. It is his task to build solidarity between them and himself. "He had to be made like his brethren, so that he might become a merciful and faithful high priest in matters which concern the relation to God, to make a plea for the sins of the people."[10]

God, on his side, by appointing an "advocate," "witness," or "redeemer" for men, has shown that man's unfaithfulness and rebellion do not put an end to his own faithfulness.[11]

2. Jesus Christ comes, demonstrating faithfulness to God and men

The coming of the Son as the defense attorney for guilty men was not what men like Peter and John the Baptist expected of the

[8] 1 Tim. 2:5; Heb. 8:6, etc. 1 John 2:1-2 speaks first of the personal advocate and only then of the instrument (*hilasmos*) that this person is for men: "We have an advocate ... and he is the sin offering [or, means of reconciliation] for our sins, and not only for our sins but for those of the whole world."

[9] Col. 2:17; Heb. 8:5; 10:1; Rom. 1:2; 3:21, 25. See Calvin's commentary on Rom. 3:25.

[10] Heb. 2:17-18; cf. 5:1-10; 7:25.

[11] Cf. the Job passages cited in note 3 above; also Rom. 3:3-4; 1 Cor. 1:9; 10:13, etc.

Messiah. As Jesus took office publicly by declaring his solidarity with penitent sinners, humbling himself, and getting baptized, the Baptist tried to "prevent" him. When Jesus announced his intention to start the journey to Jerusalem and to his execution, Peter urged him instead to save his own skin. Jesus met the obstructions of both, according to the Gospels, with echoes of Isaiah texts that speak of the fulfilment of God's righteousness and the delivering over of God's servant into the hands of the unrighteous.[12]

The Son is not only sent out by the Father and Judge to be a passive tool, as it were, of God. He also renders *obedience* to his commission by *coming* to fulfil his office. With his advent, "faith came."[13] It is not a matter of course that an attorney chosen to defend a hopeless case will actually assume the task. Still, if he is "faithful" to the one who has so directed him and "merciful" with respect to an accused whose only prospect is to perish, then he will not dodge his assignment but will do everything possible to fulfil it. Jesus Christ became "a merciful and faithful high priest," "a man sent . . . who is faithful to his creator," in short: a "faithful witness."[14] His faithfulness to God is inseparable from his love for the accused. "He loved me."[15]

God shows, by sending his Son, that he is making man's business his business; he is giving away the best and dearest he has, his Son, for the redemption of men.[16] Christ shows, equally, by accepting the office of speaker for men, that he esteems the accused so highly as to make their concerns his own. He accepts no less from God than the charge to enter into solidarity with the sinners. Thus faith in God (or better, faithfulness to God) and love for men are realized in Jesus Christ at the same time in the same deed. Faith and love in their fulness and depth are triumphant in him. Also, he shows that they are ultimately identical with each other and are therefore inseparable.

---

12 Is. 46:10; 44:28 in Matt. 3:15; Is. 53 in Matt. 17:22-23; 20:18-19.
13 Phil. 2:8; Rom. 5:19; Gal. 3:19-25.
14 Heb. 2:17; 3:1-2, 6; Rev. 1:5; 3:14.
15 Gal. 2:20; Eph. 5:2, 25.
16 Rom. 8:3, 32.

3. He confesses man's sin and reveals his predicament

The way the advocate begins his task is surprising and appears paradoxical. Instead of delivering an *apologia* for the accused, he confesses men's sins to God and pleads guilty for them. "We too [the Jews, not only the Gentiles] were, in seeking justification, found in Christ to be sinners."[17] Were Jesus in any way to contest the guilt of the inexcusable, he would be a false witness. He would be obstructing the righteousness of God and the due course of the court proceeding. He would be putting his own sincerity in a bad

[17] Gal. 2:17. This sentence, which begins in Greek with "if," is often understood as a contrary-to-fact condition (e.g., by Chrysostom; Luther, *Die deutsche Bibel*, Weimar ed., 1931, VII, 178f.; also *Luther's Works*, ed. J. Pelikan and H. T. Lehmann [St. Louis: Concordia, 1958-67], XXVI, 141-42, 145-46; R. Bultmann, "Zur Auslegung von Gal. 2, 15-18," in *Ecclesia semper reformanda*, pp. 44f.; *Zürcher Bibel*; RSV; Jerusalem Bible, etc.). If that interpretation is correct, the whole sentence affirms that Jews and Gentiles, because they are "in Christ," are by no means exposed as sinners. But a minority of interpreters, among them Calvin and E. W. Burton (*ad loc.*), believe that the condition is not contrary to fact. According to them, Gal. 2:17 contains without irony the assertion that precisely "in Christ" all men, Jews and Gentiles alike, are found guilty as sinners. At least three considerations speak for this minority view:

(1) Other sentences in Paul have analogous structures and similar content. Every time Paul rejects a deduction drawn from a premise with the words "Far be it!", he "rejects the suggested thought as one which the previous premises, themselves accepted as true, do not justify." In other words, he "accepts the premise; denies that the conclusion follows" (Burton, *Galatians, International Critical Commentary*, pp. 126f.; cf. also Burton, *Syntax of the Moods and Tenses in New Testament Greek* [Chicago: University of Chicago Press, 1893], sec. 177). Cf. Gal. 3:21a; 1 Cor. 6:15; Rom. 3:3-6, 31; 6:1-2; 7:7, 13-14; 11:1, 11. When Paul *does* formulate a contrary-to-fact condition, he likes to use the particle *an* in the apodosis (1 Cor. 2:8; 11:31; Gal. 1:10; 3:21b). This particle is missing in Gal. 2:17 (also, indeed, in 2:21; 4:15); cf. F. Blass and A. Debrunner, *A Greek Grammar of the New Testament*, tr. R. W. Funk (Chicago: University of Chicago Press, 1961), sec. 360:4. Applied to Gal. 2:17, this means that Paul accepts the premise that "in Christ" we are found to be sinners, but he rejects the conclusion that Christ is therefore a servant of sin.

(2) According to Gal. 2:15 and Rom. 3:22-23, etc., the Jews as well as the Gentiles are really and actually exposed in God's judgment as sinners.

(3) The Old Testament predecessors of the interceding Son of God quite correctly guard themselves against intending to help Israel in such a manner as to disavow or belittle her sin. On the contrary, the intercession itself reveals how great the sin is that has been committed. "Alas, this people has sinned a great sin" (Exod. 32:31). Cf. the prayer of the high priest on the Day of Atonement and the other passages cited in note 2 above.

light. The cause of his clients would be worse off after his false witness than it was before his intervention. Distortion of facts or shrewd courtroom devices cannot contribute to the saving of any client. A "true witness" (advocate) will tell the truth; in God's court he will give God the glory. Therefore Jesus Christ confesses the sins of men. His pleading is for sinful men and not for saints in disguise.

It is this confession of sin that reveals once and for all that Adam's fall is representative for and constitutive of the fall of all men. This confession binds Jews and Gentiles together in an awful solidarity: the communion of sin and guilt.[18] Because the sin of the world has been revealed in and by Jesus Christ alone, no one will succeed in proving sin by analysis or synthesis of individual or universal religious or moral misdeeds. Only the coming and the work of Jesus Christ discloses to men how bad their case is in reality. It is the Lord alone who knows his own, and he knows them better than they know themselves or each other.[19]

At this moment there is no avoiding the question whether Jesus Christ, with his outspoken confession of sin for all men, has not adopted the role of Satan in God's court. "Since we too were, in seeking justification, found in Christ to be sinners, is not Christ then a servant of sin?" Since he certainly does reveal, confess, and expose the sin of men, God's Son could indeed be seen as the executioner and destroyer of all human dignity and hope.[20] Fortunately, Christ's work of defense is not completed with the confession of guilt. This is why Paul is able to reply to the question with assurance: "Far be it!" According to the (Qumran inspired?) text of II

---

[18] Rom. 2:8-9, 11-12, 16; 3:22-23; 5:12-21.

[19] The sinfulness of all men is made clear in the Synoptic Gospels by the guilt for Jesus' death, which Jews, Gentiles, and Christian disciples all bear in their different ways. This argument is not used by Paul.

[20] In the Old Testament a political or juridical opponent is called a "satan" (1 Kings 11:14, 25, etc.). The satan who works against men before God in heaven is mentioned, e.g., in Job 1-2; Zech. 3:1-2 (cf. 1 Kings 22:21-23). The absence of a satan figure in Paul's teachings on justification is no refutation of the claim that justification has a juridical character, since the canonical prophetic indications of a last judgment give no role to Satan either. Paul refers to Satan only when he speaks of the executor of an ordained penalty (1 Cor. 5:5; cf. 10:10; 1 Tim. 1:20). This Satan adds nothing to the basic form of God's judgment upon men.

41

Corinthians 6:15, there is no harmony between or no common testimony of Christ and "Beliar." Why is Paul so certain?

4. He intercedes, and his intercession becomes a sacrifice

Jesus Christ goes on with his pleading: "He pleads for the evildoers," asking for mercy precisely because he knows their enormous guilt. "Forgive them, for they know not what they do."[21] "With loud cries and tears he carries prayer and supplication to him who can save." His last utterance is a cry.[22] May the Judge be merciful in the sight of so much guilt and misery! May he who lives and bestows life now give new life to those who are dead in sin and dead under the law! May God show himself as Father—no different from the father of the Prodigal Son, who knows well how lost and dead his son is and yet rejoices not in condemning but in forgiving and saving.

Jesus does not ask the Father to put grace before justice. Grace in the Old Testament sense (ḥen) is definitely not a dialectical antithesis to a justice that works itself out in judgment proceedings, but a synonym of divine justice. Grace means solid covenant truthfulness and special concern for a man in need of help. In being true to his covenant and his promise, God is true to himself. Even in his judging, his *judicial* concern is ultimately "setting things right" in a judicious way.[23] The speaker-for-us, Jesus Christ, knows this and therefore begs God to have mercy on the sinners. With this plea he brings together the interceding pleas of Abraham, Moses, and the high priest—and he crowns these pleas.[24] With the same prayer he

---

[21] Certain manuscripts have this reading at Luke 23:34. Ignorance of the law or of the hatefulness of a deed is, legally, not an excuse or a mitigating circumstance. Nevertheless, an accused or his advocate may bring up the fact of ignorance in order to incline the judge to clemency. Cf., e.g., Acts 17:23; 23:5; 1 Tim. 1:13.

[22] Heb. 5:7; Mark 15:37.

[23] In German, his *Richten* is ultimately to be defined as an *Aufrichten*. The New English Bible is right in translating "God's righteousness" in Rom. 1:17 by "God's way of righting wrong."

[24] Rom. 3:25. It is possible that Paul presupposes familiarity with the liturgy of the Day of Atonement on the part of his readers and therefore considers it superfluous to speak any more explicitly than he does in this verse about Christ's intercession and speaking for us.

completes his own task. "And now forgive them their sins. . . . Forgive this people their sin according to your great goodness."[25]

The intercession of the Son is not, however, confined to words and cries. Even the intercessory prayers of the Old Testament did not consist merely of sounds. Moses offered God his own life as a substitute for the life that Israel had thrown away. According to one tradition he lay fasting totally "for forty days prostrate before the Lord."[26] The high priest risked his life when he went through the curtain into the *sanctum sanctorum.* Jeremiah came to the edge of despair—or crossed over it—when he stood up for his people. Of the Suffering Servant it is said not only that he was despised, beaten, suppressed, grieved as he took the guilt of all upon himself in God's name but also that he was "cut off from the land of the living . . . struck to death."[27] For God's Son, also, when the words of intercession are spoken, the job is not yet completed. He speaks, he pleads, he begs for the sinners, louder and louder, crying, crying, crying—until he has cried himself to death. Thus, to his voice he adds his life; in biblical terminology, his blood. It was God's commission that he should be "through [his] faith a speaker-for-us in his blood"; and he has now obeyed and in fact "given himself over" in death. He did this for the accused, to whom he had directed all his love, for people who were in no way worthy of love. "He died for the godless, . . . the sinners, . . . the enemies. . . . He loved me and gave himself over for me."[28]

What effect, if any, can the poured-out blood of Jesus Christ have on the accused? Does it extinguish God's anger, reconcile God and man, give new life to man? There is no indication that it does so after the manner of consanguinity-based animistic, fetishistic, or Shintoistic models. The blood of Christ is no magical potion, no elixir of life, no natural bond of community that works automatically and overcomes lesser powers. Nor is it an *Ersatz,* bribe, or surrogate offered to God or forced on him in the place of man's forfeited life. Still less will blood serve as a payment or restitution,

25 Exod. 32:32; Num. 14:19.
26 Exod. 32:32; Deut. 9:18, 25.
27 Is. 53:8.
28 Rom. 3:25; 5:6-10; Gal. 1:4; 2:20.

as though among businessmen or under the jurisdiction of Roman law, through retribution, restitution, or substitution. Compensation may be made for damage suffered, but God is not a merchant collecting under the terms of Justinian's code. The slandering of God's honor and the dishonoring of his will that follow from sin cannot by any payment be transformed into their opposite.

But blood is able to magnify the human voice. It can show forth or call into being a totality of commitment. When a child who has been run over cries or moans from the street, the sympathy of all who have witnessed the accident is assured. But if his blood flows on the pavement, sympathy can turn into direct or immediate action in response to the misfortune or injustice that has taken place. The poured-out blood of Abel "cries" from the ground to God, and God intervenes at once. Jesus' blood "speaks even louder than the blood of Abel."[29]

All the biblical references to the blood of Jesus Christ characterize his death as a sacrifice. His death is a sacrifice in the biblical sense only because it was an act of intercession for sinners. God had willed this total intercession, and out of his faithfulness to God and his love for men, Jesus suffered death in making his plea. Indeed, several among the most outstanding sacrifices described in the Old Testament were in some way juridical acts in which God himself was entreated to make a decision accepting or rejecting the sacrificer, and in which God's judgment was pronounced.[30] The death of Jesus Christ, which marks the completion of his intercession, shows that justice and sacrifice, sacrifice and faith (or obedience), judgment and love are in no way dialectical antitheses or mutually exclusive polarities. On the contrary, they belong inseparably together where a servant of God intends to "fulfil all righteousness." He is a true

[29] Gen. 4:10ff.; Heb. 12:24.

[30] The sacrifices of Cain and Abel (Gen. 4), the sacrifice of Isaac (Gen. 22), the jealousy sacrifice (Num. 5:11-31), Hannah's sacrifice at Shiloh (1 Sam. 1), and Elijah's sacrifice on Mount Carmel (1 Kings 18:19-40) are the most important examples. G. von Rad has thrown some light on those Old Testament passages which treat of a divine verdict given on the occasion of a sacrifice; *The Problem of the Hexateuch and Other Essays* (New York: McGraw-Hill, 1966), pp. 125ff. Cf. also R. K. Yerkes, *Sacrifice in Greek and Roman Religion and Early Judaism* (London: A. and B. Black, 1953); M. Barth, "Was Christ's Death a Sacrifice?" *Scottish Journal of Theology* Occasional Papers, 9, Edinburgh, 1961.

friend, representative, and helper of man who puts his own life on the line before a judge. In his death, Jesus Christ shows a love that cannot be greater. The sacrifice of Christ is not an alternative to complete obedience to God and total love for man. It is their very sum and substance.[31]

In suffering to the death, Jesus Christ fulfils the Law and the Prophets. These require and promise only that God be loved with the whole heart and that simultaneously the neighbor be loved. Truthfulness to God reigns where mercy to the brothers triumphs. Jesus Christ obeys God by loving the neighbor. He is "the fulfilment of the law"—just as he was sent to "fulfil the requirements of the law among us."[32] He reveals his love of the neighbor by giving God his due. To "give God the glory" in the Bible means to confess one's own guilt before God and simultaneously to call on God with good confidence for mercy. The Jews and Gentiles have not done this. [33] As the only one to give God his due, Jesus shows himself to be truly man. Not at the cost of his fellow men, but at the cost of his own life, he demonstrates true humanity. True humanity is fellow-humanity. In his praying and dying he brings the human *condition* before God. In his death among men he reveals what it means to be God's image. On earth, at a definite moment, he shows that this image is not a dream or an ideal but a full and concrete reality.

Will he constrain the judge by doing this? The juridical event goes on to disclose God's sovereignty in a way that appears to be horrible.

5. The advocate is allowed to die ignominiously

God, the father of Jesus Christ, the Creator and judge of all the world, allows his Son to die—the Son who has obeyed, trusted, loved, and prayed to the death. "He did not spare his own Son, but gave him over for us all." It was God himself and no other through whom Christ "was given over for our sins."[34] When Abraham did not spare his son Isaac, God saved the boy's life. When Moses and

31 Cf. Matt. 3:15; John 13:1; 15:13; Heb. 5:7-10; 10:5-10; Ps. 51:19.
32 Mark 12:28-33; Heb. 2:17; Rom. 10:4; 8:3-4; cf. 5:19; Phil. 2:6-8.
33 Josh. 7:19; John 9:24; Rom. 3:23.
34 Rom. 8:32; 4:25; cf. Acts 2:23. The first of these verses alludes to the sacrifice of Isaac, the second to the Suffering Servant chapter, esp. Is. 53:12.

45

the high priest put their own lives in question by their sponsoring of a sinful people, God did not let them die on account of their intercession for evildoers.

The total delivering over of Christ is completed and revealed by his being hung on the cross. Although crucifixion was a Roman way of executing political agitators and seditious slaves, it also had a special meaning for Jews, who understood it as hanging on a tree. It showed that God's curse was on the one executed. On the cross Jesus suffered the death of an accursed man, of a covenant partner of God who has broken the covenant and the law.[35] He died the death that the sinners of Israel must certainly die. "Upon him was the chastisement." God has "made him who knew no sin for us become sin," he made him "bear the sins," so that he became a sin offering. Thus God has "condemned sin in the flesh": the Judgment was carried out on the body of Jesus Christ, the Son of God and the Son of David. With his death he pays "the wages of sin."[36] By doing this he sums up the history, the guilt, the chastisement of Israel. He is in person the full representative of this people.

This does not mean that the accursed Christ dies in the place of those whom he represents. On the contrary, when the king who typifies all Israel dies, every one of his servants is "crucified with him." The history of the "witness" for all contains and reveals the history of all those for whom he stands. In turn, since the Israel that Jesus Christ represents is representative of "all flesh," the whole world, every man is also "co-crucified" with Christ. Whether or not all men know yet of this death, whether or not they believe in God and in the Messiah and witness he has sent, they are legally dead. The delivering over of their advocate is fatal for them. His death is their death.[37]

---

[35] Gal. 3:10-13. In Deut. 11:26ff.; 27–30, the curse is threatened only to Israel, who is bound to God by covenant and law, and not to the nations, who were not in the covenant. Curses connected with the making of a covenant had the purpose, among other things, of preventing covert acts of disloyalty.

[36] Is. 53:5; 2 Cor. 5:21; Rom. 8:3; 6:23; cf. John 1:29.

[37] Gal. 2:19; 6:14; Rom. 6:6. Cf. E. Fuchs, *Freiheit des Glaubens* (Munich: Chr. Kaiser Verlag, 1949), pp. 28-31. It is shown especially by Rom. 5:6-8 that the "for us" of Christ's death was already in effect "while we were yet sinners." The representative function of Christ's death depends on God's commission and recognition—not on the faith and conversion of men. The

With this the proceedings before God's throne reach their most abysmal point. No wonder Jesus cries out to the Father who sent him, "My God, my God, why hast Thou forsaken me?" No wonder darkness shrouds the whole world. This is the horrible judgment of the living God. The words "anger," "curse," "sin," "cross," "crucified with him" cannot be sweetened. They cannot be relativized. They present an offense and a "scandal"[38] that cannot be removed by any wisdom, worldly or religious, and that prevent any theology from becoming a triumphal theology. In spite of Jesus' truthfulness and love, all of God's anger reigns here. Here is hellish thirst and torment, the Godforsakenness of God's own child. As Jesus made the evildoers' concerns his own, he was treated as one in solidarity with them. He became the exemplary accursed one.

God has turned against his own Son. The opposition between God and sinners, the conflict between life and death, and even the tension between fulfilment and promise is taken into God himself. In the death of his Son, God does not merely make felt what it means to bear sins and die under the curse; he feels it himself. Sin and death are no longer alien to God. Now everything that has to do with the living, obeying, hoping, achieving, doing, suffering, and dying of men has been incorporated into the relation between Father and Son. As it is manifested, it cries out to heaven. The suffering of the Old Testament prophets and men of God is not only summed up but also surpassed. The persecution and murder of Jews during two thousand years of Christian church history is anticipated. God delivers over his chosen servant. The suffering of all the innocent victims of war, hunger, and sickness has a burning focal point: instead of intervening, God permits the horrors to occur—to their bitter end.

Here God openly stands against God, the Father against the Son, the benevolent, promising God addressed in prayers, against what God makes and allows in the world of facts and events. No theoretical or doctrinal theodicy is able to break in and save the day. Even the true and loving Son can only ask, "Why have you . . . ?" In this

importance, for universal salvation, of the message of Christ and of man's faith will be discussed later.

[38] Mark 14:33-34; Rom. 1:18; 9:33; Gal. 3:13; 5:11; 6:14; 2 Cor. 5:21; 1 Cor. 1:18, 23; cf. 1 Pet. 2:8.

moment, as Jesus' last cry is raised to heaven and his blood is flowing from the cross, seemingly for no good purpose, it is possible to think about the death of God and shudder:

> Distress and dread;
> God, God is dead![39]

It is not surprising that when whole generations of God's people die by fire and the victims of bombs, napalm, hunger, and exhaustion are *in extremis*, this hellish thought comes to life again.[40]

The cry of all who still pray "My God . . . " rises to the heavens. The earth trembles. The sun fades away. This is the horror of the judgment: God is silent. An eclipse of the living God, a victory of death over life, the end of all religion, all law and justice, all morality—it is this that comes in at 3:00 p.m. on Good Friday. A Hell, deeper and hotter than anything one might imagine from myths and fairy stories about places of torment, has opened its maw, devoured God's Son, and become all-victorious.

> The one true God has let himself,
> For me, lost man and hopeless,
> Be given unto death.[41]

The judgment is adjourned at this time, to reconvene day after tomorrow at the crack of dawn.

---

[39] From a Lutheran hymn: *O grosse Not/Gott selbst ist tot!*

[40] Although F. W. Hegel spoke with ultimate seriousness about the death of God and F. Nietzsche may also have done so, this thought has, in recent times, been transmuted into the content of a salon theology and been accorded the level of seriousness of a parlor game. The holy is thrown to the hounds, and the swine have gotten hold of the pearls. Whereas for Hegel God himself, together with his history and nature, was the standard against which thought was measured, his pseudo-imitators have made modern man the measure of all things. However, Auschwitz and Vietnam are inescapable warning signs, warning us back to the core of the problem.

[41] From the hymn, *Wenn meine Sünd' mich kränken*, by Justus Gesenius: *Es hat sich selbst der wahre Gott/für mich verlornen Menschen/gegeben in den Tod.*

Interlude:

Black Thoughts About the Death

All men affected by God's judgment—pious and worldly types, religious pioneers, proud skeptics, quiet seekers, and doubt-ridden contemplatives—now have the occasion and the time to think and talk about what has happened. It is unavoidable that from the death of the only speaker-for-men, their last and only hope, a devastating conclusion is drawn. "This is our verdict: Because one has died for all, all have died. . . . I have been crucified with Christ. . . . We are planted in the same death as he. . . . You have died with Christ. . . . The world is crucified to me and I am crucified to the world."[1]

Not every death has such a comprehensive meaning. But the death of the witness installed by God *for* the accused is a catastrophe that affects the whole world.[2]

The result of the second day of Judgment is thus even worse than that of the first. Then it was sins that led to condemnation; now it is the death of him "in whom there was life," of him who came to be and to dispense the "bread of life," that effects a moral and legal death to which all men are subject.

Though possession and nonpossession of the law had earlier made a relatively significant difference in the legal standing of Jews and Gentiles, the common sinfulness and common condemnation of both had established a bond between them. Now the person and death of Christ bind them together even more strongly. "In Christ, . . . in his blood, . . . in his flesh, . . . in his body," the segregation

[1] 2 Cor. 5:14; Gal. 2:19; 6:14; Rom. 6:5; Col. 2:20.

[2] It has been said above (pp. 36f.) that the function of representing many or all men can be fulfilled only by men who are chosen by God.

49

of Jews and Gentiles is terminated once and for all; they are bound together into a unit.[3] But not everybody is happy about this kind of mediation and union. The cross itself is "a scandal to the Jews, folly to the Gentiles." The Christ whom God has abandoned has "neither form nor beauty, ... no appearance that might have appealed to us."[4]

But is there no silver lining to the cloud, no hope at all? One could say—black thoughts to the contrary notwithstanding—that God is still alive and that his thoughts are higher than ours. One could cling to the legal principle that with death the penalty for sin has been completely paid, that the reservoirs of God's wrath have been so completely emptied that at least no further judgments against sinners need be expected.[5] One might bring up some hope or other for resurrection.

But what is the use of such reflections and hopes, when God seems to behave as the enemy not only of Job but also of his own Son and of all humanity? What is gained by them when the ultimate consequence of sin—death under curse and in God-forsakenness—has come about? Certainly the highest human hope in a better hereafter has no power of its own to save men! There is nothing left to do but to "bury" all hope together with the body of Christ. By putting Jesus Christ in the tomb the very men who loved and trusted him confirm that they consider him to be truly and finally dead. "We hoped that it would be he who would set Israel free." *This* hope dies in the disciples of Jesus and is buried with him.[6] It is night. What good can the continuation of the Judgment still bring?

3 Cf. Eph. 2:11-16.

41 Cor. 1:23; Is. 53:2.

5 Rom. 6:7. The protection against double jeopardy in American law corresponds to the rabbinic-sounding sentence, "He who has died has paid the just penalty for the sin [is justified as far as that sin is concerned]."

6 1 Cor. 15:3; Matt. 27:57ff. and parallels; Luke 24:21.

The Third Day:

The Judge's Love and Power Reverse Death

1. God raises up the advocate

"On the third day" God raises his son from the dead.[1]

This raising the dead is a demonstration of the most direct personal intervention of God, of the presence of the last time, and of the fulfilment of the boldest hopes. The instrument of the awaking is the "glory," the "Spirit," or the "power" of God, which is superior to all other powers.[2] Details of the act of raising are unknown; they are not made accessible to eye witnesses or to ear witnesses. The Resurrected, however, is seen in the body by witnesses—not, indeed, "by all the people, but by the witnesses predetermined by God," who are generally called "the apostles."[3] For the Judgment to continue it suffices that the same advocate Jesus Christ, who was dead and buried, once again lives and makes a living appearance. His resurrection gives a completely new turn to the trial.

[1] 1 Cor. 15:4; Matt. 12:40; Mark 8:31; John 20:1. (It is only by accident that the third phase of our judgment narration corresponds to the biblical theme of the "third day.") The date named in the Bible is specified as being not accidental but predicted (1 Cor. 15:4). In Exod. 19:11, 16, everything that happens before the third day is mere preparation for God's complete manifestation on Sinai. Hos. 6:2 appears to be transmitting a tradition that speaks of salvation "on the third day." Cf. C. Barth, "Theophanie, Bundesschliessung und neuer Anfang am dritten Tage," Evangelische Theologie, XXVIII (1968), 521ff.

[2] Rom. 6:4; 8:10-11; Eph. 1:19-21.

[3] Gal. 1:1, 12, 15-16; 1 Cor. 9:1; 15:5-9; Acts 1:22; 10:40-41; 1 John 1:1-4, etc. What the apocryphal Gospel of Peter (35ff.) fables regarding the technicalities of Christ's resurrection reveals not only improper curiosity but also extremely poor taste. See M. R. James, The Apocryphal New Testament (London: Clarendon Press, 1955), pp. 92f.

JUSTIFICATION

In earthly juridical procedures there are analogies to the advocate
who stands up for an apparently lost cause, standing up for the
accused with words and gestures at the price, perhaps, of his reputa-
tion and even his life. In some cases he is ignored by the judge and
allowed to perish with his plea. But there are no analogies for the
resurrection from the dead. No judge has ever been able to bring a
dead man to life; the maximum of his power consists in sending live
men to their death. Neither has any court chamber been witness to
the effect of a resurrection; no verdict has been determined by one.
In God's Judgment, however, it now becomes clear why God has so
jealously kept the Last Judgment and its verdict to himself: he alone
is strong enough "to kill and make alive, conduct into Hell and bring
back out, . . . to wither a green tree and to make a withered tree
green again." He alone has the life-giving spirit at his disposal;
although earthly judges can reveal "wrath and fury" and spread
"fear and grief," only God is able to do all this and "give eternal
life, . . . glory and honor and peace."[4] For this reason God has
forbidden his people to play judge with each other, because they
would only be convicting and damning each other as they took the
administration of law and justice out of God's hands and into their
own. But "there is one lawgiver and judge: he who can *save* and
destroy. Who are you to condemn your neighbor?" For a realistic
man to judge himself would lead him only to condemn, for he does
not, like God, know "all things."[5] An earthly judge would make
himself guilty before God and men by setting a godless man free.
Now at the Last Judgment, in which God himself is the judge of all
men, including all judges, He does not intend finally to disavow the
justice that he has revealed in the Law and the Prophets. He does not
simply acquit the sinful flesh—which would be a contradiction to his
warning that the godless must not be acquitted.[6] Rather "he condemned sin in the flesh" by letting Christ die on the cross. Now

[4] 1 Sam. 2:6; Ezek. 17:24; Rom. 2:7-10. Even if enlightened judges
prescribe rehabilitation, psychiatric care, probation periods, etc., they can
only *hope for* a new life of the defendant, but not *convey* and *guarantee* it.

[5] Rom. 2:1-2; Jas. 4:11-12; 2:4; Matt. 7:1-5; 1 John 3:19-20; cf. 1 Cor.
4:3-4.

[6] See Exod. 23:7 and the passages cited in the Introduction, note 4 (p.
16).

52

he continues the juridical process by making use of his prerogative and his superior power—the power to awake the dead and to call non-being into being.[7]

What, however, is accomplished by the raising of the Son?

2. The Father proves faithful to the Son

By raising Jesus Christ from the dead, God reveals his own nature: he proves that he is faithful. In the apocalyptic literature and in the Books of the Maccabees, Jewish writers have spoken of the resurrection of the dead in the context of questions about God's righteousness, not of problems connected primarily with cosmic, metaphysical, anthropological, or psychological issues. They have waited for the time and the moment when God will demonstrate his truthfulness to those of his servants whose lives were apparently spent in vain and whose deaths were ignominious.[8] In the resurrection hopes of pious Jews, the issue was theodicy, not the continuation of human existence.[9] By resurrecting his faithful servant Jesus, God manifests his own faithfulness. Believers in God are not to think of him as an employer who lets his employees do their work and then go unpaid. Rather, "he who approaches God must believe that he . . . will be a remunerator of those who seek him."[10]

God demonstrates his truthfulness to his Son: he "justifies him in the Spirit." So, the raising of Christ is, in the first place, an intratrinitarian event. It is the Judgment of the Father concerning his obedient Son. The wording of this Judgment is no secret. It reads,

---

[7] Rom. 8:3; 4:17.

[8] E.g., Is. 26:19; Dan. 12:2; Job 19:25-27; 2 Macc. 12:42-45; Rev. 11:7-11. Passages such as Is. 26:14 and Job 14:12 show that belief in a resurrection was not held always, everywhere, or by everyone. Jesus' own disciples did not, according to Mark 9:10, belong to those (Pharisaic) circles that had clear notions and convictions in regard to resurrection. Otherwise they would not have asked, "What is resurrection from the dead?"

[9] A. T. Nikolainen, *Der Auferstehungsglaube in der Bibel und ihrer Umwelt I, Ann. Finn. Ak. Wiss.*, 49:3 (Helsinki, 1944), 156ff.

[10] Heb. 11:6. Gospel texts such as Matt. 5:12; 20:1-16; 25:14-30; Luke 17:10 show the nature of God's "remuneration." God overwhelms the unworthy with out-and-out kindness. Not all New Testament references to rewards or wages are to be understood like Rom. 4:4 as instances of belief in meritorial works (viz., "righteousness by works").

"This is [or, you are] my beloved Son, in whom I am well pleased. . . . Sit at my right hand. . . . You are a priest in eternity." A "transfiguration," seen in visions, miraculous appearances, or the ascension of Jesus Christ, confirms this judgment. The glorification and exaltation that follow the death of Jesus Christ are bound by a causal relation to the obedience which he has shown: "He was obedient. . . . *Therefore* God has exalted him." The Father has not only "given him over" but has also made it known that his Son was and always is his Son. Should one wish to separate the obedience and surrender of the Son from their recognition by God in the exaltation of Jesus Christ, one would not speak of either the Father or the Son. Jesus our Lord "was given over [by God] for our sins and raised for our justification." So faithfulness is shown to faithfulness, troth to troth, "faith to faith": truthfulness of the Son to the Father is answered by the truthfulness of the Father to the Son. [11] The giving over of the Son was not God's last word. God allows the night of terror to be followed by a new day, which in the future will be called the "day of the Lord." The light of his faithfulness shines out radiantly.

3. Christ's mediating work is justified and confirmed

The resurrection validates the works of Jesus Christ and puts them in the right light. It may have looked as if the Son had labored in vain for the evildoers, but his resurrection signifies that his works are justified, as he himself is justified. His death was a prayer. His resurrection is the answer: the intercession has been heard. His speaking-for-us is not in vain. God enthrones the speaker-for-us at his right hand so that Christ will always have God's ear. [12]

This hearing of Christ's prayer is very different from the taking of ransom money or of a fee for service. There is no thing or accomplishment that mediates mechanically or magically between God and Christ, or between God and man. [13] All mediation is effected

---

[11] 1 Tim. 3:16; Matt. 3:17; 17:5 and parallels; 2 Pet. 1:17; Acts 1:9-11; 2:34-35; Heb. 1:5-13; 2:6-9; 5:5-10; Phil. 2:8-9; Rom. 1:4, 17; 4:25; 1 Cor. 15:11ff.; 2 Cor. 5:15; 2 Tim. 2:8.

[12] Rom. 8:34; Heb. 7:25; cf. Rev. 5.

[13] The New Testament passages that treat of a ransoming and a payment

through the personal love between the Father and the Son, which in turn is inseparable from God's faithfulness to men and the compassion of Jesus Christ toward man. Out of love God does not "let his Holy One see corruption, but fills him with joy and delight." The death of his servant, suffered in full obedience, is precious in his eyes. The violent pains that he underwent are revealed as birth pangs. Thus they have a positive and creative meaning.[14]

The christological essence of resurrection is therefore this: the office performed on earth by Jesus Christ is not only acknowledged in heaven and publicized on earth but carried on in eternity. The Son of God continues to be the Lamb who bears the sins of the world, but the validity and glory of his sacrifice have now been made manifest.[15]

4. The resurrection is felt all over the world

The raising of Christ has an effect on all cosmic powers. According to the Creator's will, these powers have been determining the life and order of the world, but many men have transferred to them honor and glory due God alone. This transfer was to the powers' detriment; it led to the enslavement of man; it threatened and destroyed true worship of God and true humanity. Christ's raising is the breaking-in of God's superior power into the realm of the powers; this raising is the appearance of eternity in the realm of time and finitude, the dawn of a new eon, a devouring of death, which had been the devourer of all, a mocking of the now-broken wall that

(e.g., Mark 10:45; Gal. 3:13; 4:5; 1 Cor. 7:23; 1 Pet. 1:18-19; Rev. 1:5) do not belong to the figure of God's judgment, but are elements of a different imagery. As different metaphors and parables became confounded with one another and with the practices of Roman Law, there arose in the Middle Ages a juridical-mercantile theory of satisfaction (including the doctrine of the vicarious function of Christ and the crediting of his merits to our account), which brought forward the protests of Abelard and of later defenders of God's and Christ's love. Cf., among others, L. Hodgson, *The Doctrine of the Atonement* (New York: Scribners, 1951).

[14] Ps. 16:8-11 in Acts 2:25-28; Ps. 116:15. The meaning of "travail" sparkles in Acts 2:24; Matt. 24:8 and the texts cited in Strack-Billerbeck, *Kommentar zum Neuen Testament*, 4th ed., I (Munich: C. H. Beck'sche Verlagsbuchhandlung, 1926), 950. Cf. also John 16:21.

[15] See esp. Rev. 5.

had kept Jews and Gentiles apart; in short, it is the subjugation of all powers inimical to God and to his elect. It is God's laughing at his enemies; it is the beginning of a celebration and worship that will not only drown out the moaning of creation under its self-elected slave-drivers but also dissolve it into nothing. The raising of Jesus Christ shows forth God's freedom, his love, his constancy, his effectiveness. All creatures are touched by it and thereby freed. With the resurrection there begins a new order of all things: the new creation.[16]

5. Condemned men are raised with Christ

On the basis of the trinitarian, christological, and cosmic character of Jesus Christ's resurrection, its soteriological function becomes clear as well. "If Christ has not been raised, . . . you are still in your sins." "He was raised for our justification." "Those who live may live no longer for themselves but for him who died and was raised for them." "The life of Jesus shall be manifested in our mortal flesh." "Life is at work in you." "A new creation! The old has passed away, the new is come!"[17] What has happened is a complete change in the juridical status of everyone whom Christ has represented as advocate. When *his* intercession appeared to fail, it was *their* doom. God's anger has indeed been poured out in its fulness, but it does not last forever. The wages of sin have indeed been paid;

16 The Pauline and other New Testament assertions about the significance of the resurrection and enthronement of Christ for angels and demons (e.g., Gal. 1:4; 6:15; 1 Cor. 15:23-27, 55; 2 Cor. 5:17; 6:2; Rom. 8:19-22, 37-39; 13:1-7; Eph. 1:19-23; 4:8-10; 1 Pet. 3:21-22; Ps. 8 in Heb. 2:5-9; Ps. 2 in Acts 4:25-28; Ps. 110 *passim* in the NT) belong in themselves to the image-complex of the Messiah's enthronement and victory, and not to that of the Judgment. The enthronement complex can here only be named and not elaborated on. Nonetheless, in Rom. 8:31-39, the Judgment and lordship images are combined. See below, pp. 76-78.

17 1 Cor. 15:17; Rom. 4:25; 2 Cor. 5:15; 4:11-12; 5:17. The sermons in the early parts of Acts, which are attributed to the Jerusalem apostles, proclaim salvation and the forgiveness of sins as the effect of the resurrection of Jesus the Messiah, not of his blood or his death. This is especially clear in Acts 5:31. A similar soteriology is reflected in Paul in 1 Cor. 15:17 and Rom. 4:25b. See M. Barth, *Acquittal by Resurrection* (New York: Holt, Rinehart and Winston, 1964) for an attempt to explain the resurrection soteriology of Acts.

now they *are* paid. The death of the true witness was indeed the death of many; now his life is all the more their life! The resurrection of just anyone—of Jairus' daughter, for example, or of Lazarus—has no universal consequences for all men. But because Jesus is the one representative appointed by God for all men, his resurrection announces God's will and power to resurrect all. The dead shall live! Sinners shall be made holy! Foreigners shall become children and enemies covenant partners! God has not only willed and planned all this, but in the *same* judgment in which Jesus Christ "was given over for our sins, he was raised for our justification." Justification is resurrection: after the juridical condemnation and execution of all sinners, resurrection is the calling of all men to new life. "Awake, O sleeper, and arise from the dead, and Christ shall give you light!" Justification is creation, the new creating of man.

In the light of the resurrection of Jesus Christ, man has the freedom to say, "I have been crucified with Christ; but I live; yet it is not I who live but Christ who lives in me." He, the Messiah, is "the breath of life in our nostrils." "Christ is my life."[18] Centuries before the great Judgment a visionary writer had, in a daring manner, combined the work of the Spirit on a field of dry bones and the reunification of Judah and Israel with the raising up of a Davidic king; the three events interpret each other.[19] Precisely these events have now in combination entered the field of history: the crucified Messiah of the Jews has been raised up; Jews and Gentiles have been jointly freed from their enmity toward God and each other and united into a single people; the same Spirit through whom Christ was raised is also at work in all the limbs and members of his people. [20]

The share and the profit that the men condemned and executed with Christ have in his resurrection can be described in various ways. The accent may lie on the certainty that one day, on the Last Day, they too will rise. Alternatively, it may be emphasized that the life-giving Spirit has been given to them as a "down payment" on their inheritance and is already "at work in them." Or the bold

18 Rom. 4:25; Eph. 5:14; Gal. 2:20; Lam. 4:20; Phil. 1:21.

19 Ezek. 37 treats these apparently unrelated themes in three units that appear in sequence. Cf. vss. 1-14, 15-23, 24-28.

20 Rom. 1:3-4; 9–11; 8:11; Gal. 3:26-29; 2:20; Eph. 1:20-23; 2:1-22.

announcement is made: already "we [or, you] *are* risen."[21] This diversity does nothing to hide or diminish the common core: the resurrection of that *one* witness conveys to many a right and title to resurrection—just as the payment of an inheritance to a firstborn brother guarantees the other brothers' shares in the inheritance. Christ is "the firstborn from the dead." "We are heirs of God, namely co-heirs with Christ." His resurrection brings further resurrections in its train. What God, through his Spirit, has done to his only ("first-born") Son, through the same Spirit he will do to all his children.[22] So the effect of Christ's resurrection spreads irresistibly—not only in the successive subjugation of more and more principalities and powers, but more especially in the conferring of the Spirit on more and more men. At the same time, the different assertions about "rising with Christ" indicate that the new eon that is breaking in is not in itself the conclusion of things but a new time with a new order and a new sequence of events. Christ's rising creates not only a saving moment but also a whole period of salvation.[23]

Consequently, God's judgment is not finished with the amazement and rejoicing of the first witnesses, the apostles. The raising of the true witness and the hearing of his intercession is the unambiguous sign and solid juridical foundation for the saving of many. The "many," who eventually include the whole human race, still have to notice and acknowledge that the life given to Christ is the gift of new life to them, which can be celebrated only with jubiliation and in the joy of a new way of life. What good would God's surprising verdict, their acquittal, be for them if they become beneficiaries only passively, or even *in absentia*, knowing nothing, believing nothing, enjoying nothing?

---

21 In 1 and 2 Thessalonians and 1 Corinthians the first way is taken; the second is followed especially in 2 Corinthians and in Romans; and in Ephesians and Colossians the third is chosen. The difference may stem not only from the various problems of the congregations that Paul addresses, but also from a development and growth of Paul's thought. Cf., e.g., W. Hahn, *Mitsterben und Mitauferstehen mit Christus* (Gütersloh: Bertelsmann, 1937), and L. Cerfaux, *Christ in the Theology of St. Paul* (New York: Herder and Herder, 1966).

22 Rom. 8:11, 17, 29; Col. 1:18; Eph. 3:6.

23 1 Cor. 15:25-28; 2 Cor. 6:2.

THE JUDGE'S LOVE AND POWER REVERSE DEATH

There is an American folk song that tells of a man who stabbed someone in a moment of jealousy. Fearing what would happen at his trial, he ran away and hid in the middle of the Florida Everglades, where mosquitoes and alligators could easily find him but the sheriff's posse never could. Eventually the court heard his case *in absentia* and acquitted him on grounds of self-defense. The man was now legally acquitted, legally free. But since his friends never could find him and he never heard that he was free, he never experienced his salvation or enjoyed being free. Another man married his girl.

The judgment pronounced by God over Jews and Gentiles differs from this acquittal: the accused are declared and treated as guilty and inexcusable. "With Christ" they are delivered over to the well-deserved cross. Yet it also resembles the Everglades case insofar as the acquittal comes from God's side justly, in order, and within the jurisdiction of the court. All righteousness is fulfilled, and God has not, like Absalom and other crooked judges, simply released any and every rotten scoundrel.[24] Justification by God means, to say it again, not acquittal instead of condemnation, but raising up to new life those who have been condemned and delivered over to death.

[24] The assertion, scandalous in the light of Exod. 23:7, that God "justifies the godless" appears only once in Paul, in Rom. 4:5. Luther considered it the epitome of Paul's preaching; and Lutheran and Reformed theologians have celebrated it as the article on which the church stands or falls. See E. Wolf, "Die Rechtfertigungslehre als Mitte und Grenze reformatorischer Theologie," *Evangelische Theologie*, IX (1949-50), 298ff. (repr. in Wolf, *Perigrinatio*, II [Munich: Chr. Kaiser Verlag, 1965], 11ff.). There is no objection to this provided that it is realized that the justification of the sinner does not mean the replacement of the divine Judge with a gracious father (as in Calvin, *Institutes* III.xi.1). Cf. also P. Wernle, *Beginnings of Christianity* I (tr. G. A. Bienemann, ed. W. D. Morrison, New York: Putnam, 1903), 341ff., 35-36; Th. Zahn, *Der Brief des Paulus an die Galater* (Leipzig: A. Deichert, 1922), pp. 125f.; M. J. Lagrange, *Saint Paul: Épître aux Romains* (Paris: J. Gabalda, 1950), pp. 122ff.; C. H. Dodd, *Epistle to the Romans* (New York: Harper, 1934), pp. 118f.; O. Kuss, *Der Römerbrief*, I (Regensburg: Verlag Friedrich Pustet, 1963), 115ff.; S. Lyonnet, "Justification, Judgment, Redemption," in *Littérature et théologie pauliniennes*, pp. 178ff.; Lyonnet, "De notione justitiae Dei apud S. Paulum," *Verbum Domini*, XLII (1964), 121ff.; J. Jeremias, *The Central Message of the NT*, pp. 51ff. In the process of justification God proves to be a justly judging father. Justification is inseparable from the boon of an orderly juridical procedure. God, who prescribed a fixed order for the earthly judges of Israel, is not himself the patron of chaos.

Righteousness and life, justification and resurrection are therefore synonymous. [25]

What, then, prevents the acquittal and the life-giving *fiat* from being no more than a kind of objective datum, containing at best the possibility and the offer of salvation but not in fact reaching the men to whom new life is meant to be given?

[25] Compare Gal. 2:21 and Rom. 3:21; see also Rom. 5:10, 18; 8:10; and Hab. 2:4.

The Fourth Day:

The Verdict Is Carried Out

1. Right has might, as the Spirit demonstrates

A righteous judge makes himself responsible for seeing to it that his judgment is executed and generally acknowledged. Scandalous as it is that earthly courts are often too weak or unwilling to watch over the carrying out of a verdict, God would stand in flat contradiction to the juridical order established in his name in Israel if he were to follow up the announcement of the verdict with a retreat into inactivity. God does not retire and write his memoirs. On the contrary, he brings the judgment to its conclusion, adding new demonstrations to his previous displays of power, justice and goodness. Through the same Spirit through which he raised Christ, he lets his right and his might be sensed throughout the world.[1] Right without might would be an impotent affair. In Israel the highest juridical functions were exercised by those persons who were also equipped with power in the political and social realm. As long as they were obedient to God, judges, kings, and high priests were wise enough and strong enough to help the wronged party obtain victory. It is not for nothing that for the prophets, the Psalmists, and the apocalypticists, the establishment of God's royal hegemony and the victory of his righteousness are one and the same event.[2] The one great Judgment of justification includes God's action in making the

[1] This is treated in numerous passages that speak (to translate literally) of God's undiminishing "energy," i.e., his continuing, palpable action and influence, e.g., Gal. 2:8; 3:5; 1 Cor. 12:6; Phil. 3:21; Col. 1:29; Eph. 1:11; 3:7, 20.

[2] The close connection between right and might is emphasized especially in the essay of E. Käsemann and in the books of his students P. Stuhlmacher and C. Müller mentioned in the note on the literature.

61

righteousness of the Judgment felt and making the gloriousness of his verdict shine out. His power goes out into the wide world just as effectively as it infiltrates the chaos of social relationships and reaches down into the abyss of the soul. As God's power demonstrations are carried out by his *Spirit*, he reveals the unity of Father, Son and Holy Spirit. Not only the Father and the Son, but also the Holy Spirit is at work wherever justification is at issue.[3]

2. Judgment becomes gospel and constables become apostles

The work of the Spirit has a cognitive aspect. The Spirit reveals God's righteousness to certain men. He equips and appoints them to go out into all the world, among the circumcised Jews as well as among the uncircumcised nations, and make God's gracious Judgment known.[4] The Judgment itself, but also the act of proclaiming it, is called, following Isaiah, "gospel," "evangel," that is, good news.[5] The bearers of this message, who are authorized messengers of the divine court, are called "apostles." They owe their title (wholly or in part) to the institution of deputized agents of the Jewish courts. The message that these men, commissioned and sent by Christ, are to circulate does not consist of naked words but shows itself, even far away in space and time, as the effectual, present "power of God for salvation. . . . For his verdict [or, his Judgment, his righteousness, his justification, his procurement of salvation] is revealed in it." Through the gospel, God himself "makes his salvation known; he reveals his righteousness before the eyes of the nations."[6]

This means that when the apostles go to deliver the message much more happens than the initiation of a cognitive process, and more is accomplished than men could accomplish. The same Spirit through whom Christ was raised and the apostles illuminated falls on the

3 In, e.g., Gal. 3:2, 5; 5:6; 1 Cor. 6:11, and 1 Tim. 3:16, justification is attributed, entirely or in part, to the Spirit of God.

4 1 Cor. 2:9-16; Gal. 1:12, 15-16; 2:7-9.

5 Is. 40:9; 52:7; 60:6; 61:1; cf. Ps. 40:9, "I proclaimed his righteousness in the great congregation"; Ps. 96:2, "Tell of his salvation from day to day"; Gal. 1:16; Rom. 1:1; 15:16, etc.

6 Rom. 1:16-17; Ps. 98:2.

listener while the gospel is preached. New life sprouts up from the ruins of souls, of homes, and of a thousand interpersonal relationships where sin and death had previously reigned. In this way the proclaiming apostle and those addressed receive proof together from God that the authority of the apostles, the content of their preaching, and the faith of the hearers are not a matter of humans and human wisdom. A "demonstration of the Spirit and of power" takes place where the gospel is proclaimed with God's blessing.[7] In this way the preached gospel, the apostolate and the congregations which now arise demonstrate the power of the divine Judge and the validity of his Judgment.

Not only the fact but also the quality of apostolic existence proves that God's Judgment is implementing itself. The content of the Judgment message is mirrored and made credible in the lives and life stories of the bearers and receivers of the message. The preaching of Christ crucified and resurrected is reflected in the suffering and weakness of the apostle, who comes more and more to be "formed like" the crucified and day by day remains dependent on the life and the power promised and brought to him by God. The same thing is true for the new congregations and for each of their members.

The Judgment character of the preached gospel is made public not only in the regular references to the trial, execution, and resurrection of Jesus Christ but also when the apostles must become "witnesses" before earthly potentates and courts. The one "true witness" is followed by a train of "witnesses." The whole world, represented by its potentates—especially public places of assembly, including the temple in Jerusalem, synagogues, imperial and religious courts—becomes the setting for the proclamation of God's Judgment and an exhibition of its validity.[8] God lets all powers not only know

---

[7] Gal. 3:1-5; 1 Cor. 2:3-5; 2 Cor. 3:1-3; cf. Acts 10:44-47; 11:15-18; 15:8-9. Concerning the following paragraph, see esp. Phil. 1:21; 3:10, 21, etc.; 2 Cor. *passim;* Rom. 8:17-18; Gal. 4:19; 6:17; cf. 1 Pet. and Rev. *passim.*

[8] Four elements of the New Testament writings probably stand in a covert relation to Paul's doctrine of justification:

(1) The key position that the account of Jesus' trial assumes in the Gospels.

(2) The announcement that the apostles must bear their witness before kings and governors and there be inspired by the Spirit in order to give this witness at all.

his judgment but also feel it. Like the apostles, they will have to submit themselves to the Lord of all lords and put themselves at his service.[9]

3. The Judge receives praise, which is faith

God does not stop with the communication and imposition of his justice. In every legal procedure it is not only the accused who is on trial. The accuser is on trial; the court system, the law, justice—perhaps personified as a goddess—are on trial; and in a special way even the judge is on trial. It may happen that everyone who is immediately affected by a sentence passed or who just hears about it must cry out, "That's not right!"[10] If such a reaction is produced, what good is the judge's legal erudition, and what good is his power? At any rate, God's righteousness and his treatment of men in his court move the multitude of persons affected by it to break out into a doxology:[11]

Thou art right [lit., justified] in Thy sentence
and blameless in thy Judgment (Ps. 51:4; Rom. 3:4).

O the depth of the richness and the wisdom
and the knowledge of God! (Rom. 11:33).

He is right! (Is. 41:26).

(3) The account in the Book of Acts, according to which the preaching of the gospel leads from one city and courtroom to another, and is not hindered by apparent straits and roadblocks but rather is powerfully furthered.

(4) The references to the Last Judgment, which is to come.

Philippians, which refers to justification explicitly in 1:1; 3:6, 9, unites all these elements. It is improbable that the various New Testament statements about this or that judgment are fundamentally different from what Paul expresses in his doctrine of justification. For this reason, non-Pauline texts have been combined with Pauline passages in this essay in order to clarify Paul's doctrine.

9 1 Cor. 9:16-17; 15:25; Rom. 8:37-39; 13:4; Phil. 2:10-11.

10 In Rom. 3:5; 9:14, Paul rules out the possibility of attributing unrighteousness to God.

11 Exclamations such as this are called Judgment doxologies, Gerichtsdoxologien. See above, note 11, p. 20, for more examples.

The Old Testament does more than record individual voices making such confessions. It also describes solemn days and feasts at which the whole people, responding to God's acts of election, liberation, and self-revelation, make a confession and obligate themselves. According to the Deuteronomic (perhaps also to an ancient "amphyctyonic") tradition, a kind of loyalty oath completes the juridical process of covenant-making between God and his people. "You have declared this day concerning the Lord that he is your God. . . . And the Lord has declared this day concerning you that you are a people for his own possession. . . . This day you have become the people of the Lord your God."[12]

The same prominent place that belongs to the making of the covenant between God and Israel in the Old Testament belongs to God's Judgment over Jews and Gentiles in Paul. The Apostle does not diminish the meaning of the covenant. He knows what Jeremiah foretold; he knows the early church's tradition of Old and New Covenant;[13] but the concepts of righteousness and Judgment are more important to him than an elaboration of the concept of covenant. Still, as with the covenant, God's judgment and verdict want to be accepted by men, acknowledged as right and valid, and attested by a certain way of life. God himself wishes to be acknowledged and praised by men of their own free will. He does not want to rule over them like a puppeteer over marionettes or a dictator over sycophants, but rather like a father ruling over his children.

The name Paul gives to the doxology or exhomologesis expected and produced by God is simple and straightforward: Paul calls it *faith*. The doing and deciding, the living and suffering that express the proper praise of God are denoted by a verb meaning "to believe" or "to live in faith."[14] What God expects of those who get word of

---

12 Esp. Deut. 26:5-11, 16-19; 27:9-10; 29:10-15; Josh. 24. See K. Baltzer, "Das Bundesformular," *Wissenschaftliche Monographien zum Alten und Neuen Testament* 4 (Neukirchen, 1960). It is precisely the forensic character of the enactment of the covenant that calls for an actual answer from the people and an alteration in their way of life. The obligations expected of God's people and taken up by them contradict the assumption that this people could and should merely behave "as if" it were elected and made holy.

13 Rom. 9:4; Eph. 2:12; 1 Cor. 11:25; 2 Cor. 3:6.

14 1 Cor. 15:11, etc.; Gal. 2:20. H. Ljungmann comes close to equating faith with doxology; *Pistis* (Lund: C. W. K. Gleerup, 1964), pp. 38ff.

his Judgment is nothing other than the behavior that was, in the Old Testament, the mark of a faithful covenant partner.[15] He who accepts God's promise, covenant, and justice as right and is pleased with them, he who stands unshakably on this foundation, he who builds, acts, waits, suffers, hopes, and serves on this foundation—*believes.* Steady compliance with the covenant and loyalty to God and the brothers, or, more simply, *faithfulness* is the "faith" of the Old Testament. This faith—together with love, fear, righteousness, and truth—is the only possible response to the faithfulness, love, grace, righteousness, and truth with which God holds fast to his election, his words of promise, and his covenant. The same way of life should be the human response to God's final judgment: a "life in the faith of [or, faith in] him who loved me."[16] A trusting faithfulness on man's part is the right answer to the faithfulness God has shown in sending and resurrecting the intercessor. Believing means taking refuge in Jesus Christ's obedience and love, that is, in his faith. It means to live from it, with it, and according to it. Jesus Christ's faith is so great and comprehensive that man is safe under the protection of its wings. "In Christ" man is justified by faith.

Believing does not stand primarily in contrast to seeing, to reasoning, to doubting, or to living. Rather it is the opposite of disobedi-

---

15 On the basis of Pauline passages such as Gal. 3:23, 25 which equate the date of the "coming of faith" with that of Jesus Christ's coming, it has been argued that the justifying faith Paul proclaims is different from the *emunah* (faith, faithfulness) of the Old Testament servants of God. See A. Richardson, *An Introduction to the Theology of the New Testament* (New York: Harper, 1958), pp. 19ff. The Epistle to the Hebrews, which presupposes and proclaims the identity of Old Testament and New Testament faith, is read by E. Grässer, e.g., as outspokenly un-Pauline; *Der Glaube im Hebräerbrief* (Marburg: N. G. Elwert, 1965). This is contradicted, however, by Paul's using Old Testament men and Old Testament passages to illustrate and explicate the nature and power of faith to his Christian readers. In particular, he refers to Gen. 15:6; Is. 28:16; Hab. 2:4 repeatedly; see Rom. 4, Gal. 3 and Rom. 10. According to Paul, faith is not a completely novel posture, since Abraham was justified by faith (Gal. 3:6-9; Rom. 4:1-22)! That which was reported about him "was written for our sake too" (Rom. 4:23-24). In the New Testament is added an unheard-of extension, clarity, and glory to the contents and promises of the Old Testament (2 Cor. 3:10); but it does not introduce a mode of justification unknown or contrary to the things "attested by the Law and the Prophets" (Rom. 3:21).

16 See, e.g., Exod. 34:6; Hos. 2:19-20; Gal. 2:20.

ence to and denial of God, of unfaithfulness and refusal to obey, of a life led on precarious and shifting ground.[17]

The "reckoning of faith as righteousness" is not a matter of bookkeeping, not a matter of carrying over an alien credit into an overdrawn bank account, surely not a matter of treating a man according to the fiction that he is in the right. Rather, it is the expression of the pleasure that God takes·in a man's complete trust and obedience. Seeing the faith of his chosen, God confirms his gracious decision: he "plans" faithfully, viz. "in righteousness," to carry out his promise at the proper time.[18]

[17] Only a marginal role is played by the opposition between seeing and believing or the corresponding opposition (suggested by Greek philosophy) between faith and knowledge; see 2 Cor. 5:7; 1 Cor. 1:18ff.; 13:12; cf. Heb. 11:1; 1 Pet. 1:8;|John 20:29.

Or should the usual translations of Rom. 4:20; 14:23; Matt. 21:21; Mark 11:23; and Jas. 1:6 demonstrate that doubt is the opposite of faith? Passages like Acts 10:20; 11:2; Jas. 2:4 show that the middle (and the aorist passive; see Blass-Debrunner, *A Greek Grammar of the New Testament*, tr. R. W. Funk [Chicago: Univ. of Chicago Press, 1961], sec. 78) of the Greek verb most often translated "doubt" actually meant, in New Testament times, "answer," "decide," "contest," or "set oneself up as judge" (see the lexicons, e.g., tho﹐. of W. Bauer and of Liddell and Scott, s.v. *diakrinomai*). Whence would the different New Testament writers have suddenly and simultaneously acquired the boldness and confidence to impose the meaning "doubt" on a word that had never (demonstrably) possessed this meaning before? The Hebrew language has no word for "doubt." In good Greek, other words are used to mean "doubt" than the one that appears in the passages cited above. Only in writings later than the New Testament is the verb used in Rom. 4:20, etc., unambiguously understood as the psychic posture of doubting. Under the influence of this development, the nature of faith was also narrowed down and restricted to the sphere of psychology and epistemology. The ethical and social character of faith was lost.

The contrast between faith and life or between faith and works (e.g., Jas. 2:14-26) can puff itself up and infect the church only in those places where Paul's joining of faith and love (Gal. 5:6, 13-14; 1 Cor. 13:13; Eph. 1:15; 3:16-17, etc.) is unknown or forgotten. The faith that comes from hearing (Is. 53:1; Rom. 10:16-17) stands in opposition to the response of a "disobedient and contradicting people" (Is. 65:2; Rom. 10:21). That faith means standing fast is clear in passages like Is. 28:16 and 65:2, quoted in Rom. 9:33 and 10:21, and also in Rom. 3:4; cf. Heb. 3:12–4:3; 1 Cor. 16:3; Col. 1:23; 2:5, 7; Eph. 4:13-14; Heb. 10:39; Jas. 1:6, etc. The New Testament writers obviously enjoy alluding to the root (which means "be firm") of the Hebrew word for faith.

[18] Gen. 15:6; Rom. 4:3-6, 9, 22-24; Gal. 3:6; Jas. 2:23; and, especially, Gen. 50:20 show that the verb ("reckon") used in Gen. 15:6 and quoted by Paul can mean "plan." We may speak of a wrapping-up of man's faith in God's

"Justified by faith"[19] means, accordingly, tried by the faithful God, sentenced conformably to the appearance, death, and rising of the obedient and loving Son, acquitted and set free in a manner identical with new creation and recognizable only with rejoicing and thanksgiving. God's faith, the faith of Jesus Christ, and man's answer in faith are—each in its own way—the means by which righteousness and life are given to the community of sinful Jews and Gentiles.

It is true: man is justified *sola fide*, by faith alone. But this saving faith is much more than a mere existential posture and response of man. Faith is first of all the characteristic and gift of God and his Son. Built on the faithfulness of the Judge and the Advocate, human trust and faithfulness toward God stand on firm ground. There is no other requisite or means of justification beyond this. It would be quite ludicrous, in the light of the righteousness revealed and demonstrated by God, for a man to claim that man can become righteous by means of his own perfectibility or perfection, that the law is strong enough to make him righteous, or that certain commandments, singled out and fulfilled to the letter, should of some necessity satisfy God and be reckoned as meritorious. The Judge is not a trader. He yields neither to cash offerings nor to other bribes. Rather, "Jesus Christ was made wisdom for us by God, [that is, was made] righteousness, holiness and redemption." This proposition is synonymous with the confession: "Man is justified by faith alone."[20]

promise. Upon God's promise, Abraham believes. Abraham's faith, in turn, is confirmed by the carrying out of the promise and plan of God. Faith is the right acceptance of the promise; it is the beginning and sign of its forthcoming fulfilment.

[19] Gal. 2:16; Rom. 3:28, etc.

[20] Rom. 3:28; Gal. 2:15-21; 1 Cor. 1:30-31; Phil. 3:4-11. On one occasion Luther defined the relation between justification *by* God and justification *of* God through faith in the following way: "[God] changes us into his Word, but not his Word into us. He makes us righteous and true when we believe that his Word is righteous and true. Then the same character is possessed by his Word and the believer, i.e., truth and righteousness. When he is justified, he justifies, and when he justifies, he is justified. . . . God's passive and active justification and our faith or trust in him are one and the same." See *Luthers Vorlesung über den Römerbrief* 1515-16 (ed. J. Ficker; Leipzig: Dieterich'sche Verlagsbuchhandlung, 1908), "Scholien," pp. 65-66; cf. the translation of W. Pauck, *Luther: Lectures on Romans* (Vol. 15, *Library of Christian Classics*, Philadelphia: Westminster, 1961), pp. 77-78. For a commentary on these words,

4. Faith takes form in community and love, in confession and joy

As the praise of Judge and Judgment resounds in lives of faith, there is no end to the forms it takes. Still, there are a few constants:

There is no acceptance and praise of God's judgment except by a congregation in which different people and groups are united. The divine juridical pronouncement (the gospel) calls men who were previously divided and alienated into a community. The case of Jews and Gentiles, rich and poor, male and female has been heard on the same day. Both have not only been condemned but also welded together at the same time, by Jesus Christ's intercession, into a unity of guilt and forgiveness. Therefore the celebration evoked by God's verdict can only be a common celebration. Because of God's Judgment, Jews and Gentiles are "one in Christ," "at one," "one single new man." As such they cannot separate themselves from one another, "exclude" each other, or wish to outdo each other. Rather they will carefully preserve the "unity of the Spirit in the bond of peace" and oppose vigorously any segregationist tendencies such as those which became visible in Antioch, threatened in Galatia, and broke out into the open in Rome over questions of menu. Mutual love, which "bears all things," is the form in which Christians seek to fulfil God's commandment and will. Their whole ethics and morality stand under the rubric of this love.[21] To be in Christ means for them the same things as life in that community of love which is the congregation. Therefore, they praise God "in the church and in Christ Jesus." Only "together" with brothers does any member of the church have "access to the Father."[22]

The communal form of response and praise called forth by God's Judgment includes personal acts inside, at the periphery of, and outside the community. To these acts belong (a) turning away from

see J. H. Iwand, "Gottes Gerechtigkeit nach Luthers Lehre," *Theologische Existenz Heute*, LXXV (1941), 11ff.

[21] Gal. 2:3-5, 11-14; 3:29; 4:17; 5:13—6:10; 1 Cor. 12—14; Rom. 13:9-10; Col. 3:11-15; Phil. 3—4; Eph. 4—6. It is hardly an accident that justification by faith alone, the unity of Jews and Gentiles and fulfilment of the law through love and peacefulness are always treated together in Paul's letters and are always treated in the same order.

[22] Eph. 3:21; 2:18; 3:12; Matt. 18:19-20. Cf. the meaning of mutual forgiveness in Matt. 5:23-26; 6:12, 14-15; 16:19; 18:18, 21-35; John 20:22-23; Jas. 5:19-20.

evil ways and turning toward the Lord ("conversion," so called); (b) joining in the confessions: "Jesus is Lord!" "God is one!" "One Spirit!"; (c) praying to God as "Our Father"; (d) Singing hymns of praise; (e) exhorting and consoling brothers in "a spirit of meekness"; and (f) giving account to outsiders of one's faith.[23] The fulness and value of the praise is in no way diminished by the fact that its form is prominently verbal: God's praise is first of all spoken and sung (in the case of apostles, evangelists, and seers, also written) in various modes of prayer, proclamation, confession, and hymnody. The mouth runs over with what the heart is full of. By no means is it beneath the dignity of the God who reveals himself in words and the men who have been reached by these words that they now should bear witness with proper words to the fact that God is just. The "fruit of the lips" is a "praise offering," acceptable to God.[24]

Nevertheless, the praise of God is not entirely verbal. The congregation's love and its upbuilding take precedence even over all too many prophetic words (1 Cor. 12–14). Thankfulness to God will be expressed by everyone "with hearts and hands and voices." Where God is praised in this way, his judgment is brought to completion and the goal of the gracious judgment is reached. Thus it is demonstrated that justification is not merely a pronouncement, let alone an offer or a possibility, but includes in itself the salvation of the individual and his new life. It effects what it offers. Conversion, confession, prayer, and song are proofs that the Judge has carried the demonstration of his saviorhood deep into the communal life of men and into the hearts of individuals. The acquitted live as persons saved and rejoice in their new life.[25]

[23] (a) 1 Thess. 1:9; 2 Cor. 3:16; cf. Gal. 1:13-24; Phil. 3:3-14; (b) 1 Cor. 8:6; 12:3; Rom. 10:9; Eph. 4:4-6; (c) Gal. 4:6; Rom. 8:15; (d) Col. 3:16; Eph. 5:19; (e) Rom. 1:12; Gal. 6:1; (f) 1 Pet. 3:15, etc.

[24] Heb. 13:15.

[25] Luther, in translating the Greek "be saved" (e.g., in 1 Cor. 1:18; Rom. 10:9; and Eph. 2:5, 8) with *selig werden* (become happy or blessed), gave beautiful weight to the personal and subjective character that distinguishes this verb in Paul (but not in the Old Testament and elsewhere) from the more public and social character of "be justified."

5. The Judgment is celebrated in baptism and the Lord's supper

Especially solemn occasions of the Judgment celebration are baptism and the Lord's supper. Insofar as both belong under the rubric of lived faith and judgment doxology, it can be asserted that man is justified in baptism and in the supper. Each in its own way is a public and binding expression of that faith which, as the answer to God's and Christ's faith, is inseparable from justification.

The juridical character of baptism, before the coming of the Messiah and before the Judgment executed in his presence, consisted in its being a plea: the baptized declared himself guilty in the face of the coming Judge and Judgment and confessed his sins. There was, according to John the Baptist's message, no other way to ask "for forgiveness." Indeed John's baptism with water was a preparation for another washing; it was an entreaty for the purification that God alone can bring about with "pure water," i.e., the Holy Spirit. After Pentecost, the baptism administered in the Christian congregation is described in similar terms: repentance, confession of sins, prayer for the Holy Spirit, faith are its essential features. On one occasion baptism is defined as a "prayer [or, application] to God for a good conscience."[26] In the light of Jesus Christ's crucifixion and death, baptism is also interpreted as a burial: those who (in consequence of God's Judgment!) "know that they have died with Christ" allow themselves to be treated in baptism as dead men: "By baptism we are buried with him. . . . You are buried with him in baptism."[27] Baptism is thus an act that gives a confirmation carried out by the baptized, the baptizer, and the congregation. It confirms God's sentence of death and man's acceptance of it. But it is not just this! Baptism is at the same time an attestation of hope in the resurrection. This is both desired and done "so that as Christ was raised from the dead by the glory of the Father, we too might walk in newness

---

[26] Luke 7:29; 3:2-20; Matt. 3:1-13; Mark 1:1-8; Acts 2:38; 1 Pet. 3:21. In Ezek. 36:25-27, the Spirit of God is characterized as the purifying water that goes to the heart; in the Qumran text of Is. 52:15, the Suffering Servant is characterized as he who will "sprinkle" [with the Spirit?] even the Gentiles.

[27] Rom. 6:4; Col. 2:12. "Burial with him" has nothing to do with burial in water, e.g., through baptism by immersion. For a Jewish author immersion in water could never signify a burial. The metaphor of burial refers to the meaning of baptism, not to its form.

of life." "In him you are circumcised. . . . In him you are also raised up."[28] He who knows this and, believing, is willing to attest it, asks for baptism and receives it. "They justified God [acknowledged his rightness] by being baptized."[29]

The Lord's supper is a feast of thanksgiving and joy. In anticipation of the glorious return of Jesus Christ, those assembled celebrate above all the power of the Lord's death, which sustains the community and guarantees peace with God and men.[30] This does not make the eucharist a ceremonial commemoration of a deceased person, and certainly not a burial rite. It is not a past Lord, but the present and coming Lord who is celebrated. It is not the expiration of his rule but the present power of his Spirit that forms the context of the supper. Precisely where demonstrations of the presence of the Spirit are characteristic of a congregation, the celebration of the Lord's supper stands under God's Judgment; and the celebrants attest the validity of God's Judgment and their acceptance of it. How does this happen? The supper of the Lord tolerates no separation of rich from poor, of strong from weak, of persons who eat everything from ascetics. If a separation does take place, or if a part of the congregation tries to force its view on the others, then Christ's body and blood are insulted, the community that Christ founded is belied, and the blasphemers come under condemnation. A man can "eat and drink judgment upon himself." The congregation has the experience that unworthy participation in this feast of love has consequences for morals, for health, and even for life itself. Because the table fellowship belongs to the Judgment of God that is still going on, sickness, weakness, rebukes, humiliations, and even death occur in the congregation. They are God's "chastisements." They reveal what it means to dishonor the living, present Lord.[31]

Even while the Judge is praised and the Judgment is celebrated, God keeps the Judgment in his own hands and refuses to be mocked.

[28] Rom. 6:4, Col. 2:11-12.

[29] Luke 7:29.

[30] 1 Cor. 10:16-17; 11:23-26; 16:22; Acts 2:42, 46-47; Rev. 3:20-21; cf. Eph. 2:14-16.

[31] Gal. 2:11-14; 1 Cor. 11:27-34, esp. vss. 29, 32; Rom. 14:13-23. Cf. C. F. D. Moule, "The Judgment Theme in the Sacraments," in W. D. Davies and D. Daube, ed., *The Background of the New Testament and Its Eschatology*, in honor of C. H. Dodd (Cambridge: The University Press, 1956), pp. 464ff.

"He who stands, let him look lest he fall!" Let no man set himself up as a judge over his neighbor! It is precisely God's elect who have to bear the greatest tests and temptations. They should not be upset about this, but learn to consider this: the Judgment begins with God's house, and God does not impose a test that is too hard.[32]

No information is given concerning how long such tests or temptations will last. What is certain is that they will come to an end. The fourth day of God's Judgment extends from Pentecost to the glorious second appearance of Jesus Christ. Even though all who live in awareness of this day are still living "in the flesh," they are not bound to live "according to the flesh" and to accomplish "works of the flesh." "Driven by the Spirit," they bring forth "the fruit of the Spirit." The day of continued conflict against evil—of tension between the already given and the not yet achieved—is God's day as much as are the other days of the Judgment.[33] This day is not yet over. It is the time of the gospel, which still wants to run and spread itself further abroad. It is the day of faith, in which still more men must come to know about their salvation and be happy about it. It is the time of the church that celebrates already, though it is under stress and struggles. This day, in turn, calls for a fulfilment and a completion for which it is still open. Therefore it is a day of waiting, hurrying, hoping. The substance and embodiment of hope is the exalted Jesus Christ himself.[34]

[32] 1 Cor. 10:1-13; 1 Pet. 1:6-9; 4:12-19.

[33] Gal. 2:20; 3:3; 5:16-25; 2 Cor. 6:2; 10:2-3; Rom. 8:5-16; Eph. 4:13; 6:10-20, etc. O. Cullmann has described this tension most eloquently (e.g., in *Salvation in History*, tr. S. G. Sowers, *et al.* [London: SCM Press, 1967]).

[34] Col. 1:5, 27; Mark 13:10; 2 Pet. 3:9; Rev. 6:11; Phil. 3:12-14. "Through the Spirit, by faith, we wait for the hope of righteousness" (Gal. 5:5). "In hope we are saved" (Rom. 8:24; cf. Luther, *ad loc.:peccatores in re, justificati in spe*). It is characteristic of Galatians that (apart from the case of Abraham, Gal. 3:6) justification is spoken of only in the present and future tenses and in corresponding aorist subjunctives, but is never spoken of as an event completed in the past. See, e.g., Gal. 2:16-17, 21; 3:8, 11, 21, 24; 5:4-5. In Romans, on the other hand, in addition to statements about the present and future Justification (2:13; 3:20, 24, 26; 5:19; 8:33), there is the retrospective formulation: "We have been justified.... God has justified" (5:1, 9; 6:7; 8:30).

The Fifth Day:

The Last Day Is Still to Come

1. The Judgment will be in the hands of Jesus Christ

Many faithful members of Israel had placed their hopes in the coming and triumph of the promised Messiah. This hope was confirmed in the sending and raising of the true witness Jesus Christ. It was, in exemplary fashion, already fulfilled between Easter and Pentecost when it "glowed" in the hearts of the faithful. But not only then and there! The New Testament affirms that this same hope is enthroned bodily at the right hand of God and permeates the church on earth;[1] this "hope does not disappoint us."[2] The day that brings the crowning fulfilment of all promises is distinguished from earlier phases of the divine Judgment by the fact that it begins with Jesus Christ's appearance before the whole world. On this day he carries out in God's name the Judgment that had previously been called God's Judgment rather than Jesus Christ's, namely, righteousness. Now he who served as man's witness and advocate takes the office of Judge. "God will ... judge through Jesus Christ." In the coming Judgment the good or evil works done by man will play a great role: "Before the judgment seat of Christ, ... each one will receive good or evil, according to what he has done in the body."[3]

[1] Luke 24:52; Col. 1:27; 3:1-4.

[2] Rom. 5:5; cf. Is. 28:16 (LXX).

[3] Paul's statements about the coming judgment according to works (2 Thess. 1:5-10; Gal. 6:5, 7-10; 1 Cor. 3:13-15; 2 Cor. 5:10; 11:15; Rom. 2:5-13; Eph. 6:8; cf. 2 Tim. 4:7-8, etc.) are sometimes looked on as being incompatible with his doctrine of justification by grace and faith alone without works of the law. B. Weiss (in H. A. Meyer's *Kritisch-Exegetischer Kommentar über das NT,* 7th ed. [Göttingen: Vandenhoeck und Ruprecht,

The final day or Last Judgment is an essential part of the justification Judgment; it is not a mere appendage, not a competing judicatory or a judicial review.

The appearance of the risen Christ on the third day took place before only a few selected witnesses. In the time span between Easter and the Last Day, men were referred to the dynamic manifestation of the Spirit and the real but not yet palpable presence of the Lord. Life itself was hidden in God, even when the Messiah had his effect as "the breath of life in the nostrils" of the congregation and its members.[4] The Last Day, however, brings before all flesh the visible appearance of life, the glorification of Jesus Christ, his power, his work, his honor. "All flesh must see God's salvation." To the extent that, in the intervening period, "believing"[5] was less than

1886], pp. 113-114; but see H. Braun's work cited in the note on the literature) cautions against relating Rom. 2:5ff. to the doctrine of justification and suggests that the notion of a judgment according to works is a relic of Paul's pre-Christian thinking, betraying a propensity toward works-righteousness. But according to 2 Thess. 1:7; 1 Cor. 4:5; 2 Cor. 5:10; Phil. 4:4-6; Rom. 2:16; Col. 3:4 (cf. Matt. 7:21-23; 25:31-46; 1 John 3:2; Rev. 5:8-12; 19:1-16, etc.) it is none other than "our Lord Jesus Christ," the "slaughtered lamb," the "true witness" who "appears in glory" and who, "before God's judgment seat," brings that "righteous judgment of God" to completion which, according to Rom. 2:5; 14:10, is God's own Judgment. Since Paul explicitly asserts that the judgment according to works is placed in the hand of (the crucified and risen) Jesus Christ, it is impossible to hold the position that Paul's assertions about the Last Judgment are directly derived from "Jewish" imagery and not influenced by his faith in Jesus the Messiah. Several recent interpretations of Paul (e.g., K. Stalder, *Das Werk des Gesetzes in der Heiligung bei Paulus* [Zurich: EVZ Verlag, 1962], pp. 258ff., 455ff.; R. Bring, *Commentary on Galatians*, tr. E. Wahlstrom [Philadelphia: Muhlenberg, 1961], pp. 130, 241, 275ff.; E. Jüngel, *Paulus und Jesus* [Tübingen: Mohr, 1964], pp. 66-70; cf. "Zum Verständnis der Vorstellung vom Gericht nach den Werken in Röm. 2,2-11," *Zeitschrift für Theologie und Kirche*, LX [1963], 70ff.) correctly emphasize that justification through works of the law on the one hand, and judgment according to works on the other are fundamentally different things. Therefore, justification without works of the law and judgment according to works do not exclude each other but have to be explained as complementary. Rom. 2:5-16 and 3:21-31 belong together just as much as 1 Cor. 1:30 and 3:13-15; 4:5. See also K. Stendahl, "Justification and Last Judgment," *Lutheran World*, VIII (1961), 1ff.

[4] Lam. 4:20; Gal. 2:20; Phil. 1:21; Col. 3:3; Eph. 3:17. From his heavenly throne, the "head" confers life and growth on his "body," the church (Eph. 1:20-23; 4:15-16).

[5] In the Greek sense of the word as opposed to the Hebrew. Cf. 2 Cor. 5:7 and the passages cited in note 17, p. 67.

"seeing" and signified no more than a preliminary type of knowledge and acknowledgment of God and his Judgment, faith is now both validated and superseded by an appearance and immediate knowledge of God that leaves nothing hidden on either God's side or man's side. On this day God and his Messiah are open to view for the first time: "I will know as I am known." "We will see him as he is." "Every eye will see him, even those who pierced him."[6] Thus the Last Day is the day of the glorification of Jesus Christ; it is his day, the epitome of the "day of the Lord." The meaning of the day is most of all christological. *Christus victor!* The slaughtered Lamb appears as the lion who overcomes all and is worthy of the highest honor.[7]

In the light of this day all previous days, especially the immediately preceding time, are "evil days" or an "evil day." The time before the end would have been unbearably long were it not graciously shortened. The day that comes, however, guarantees and brings its end.[8]

2. Heaven and earth will be created anew

Like the resurrection, Christ's final glorious appearance is of cosmological import. Not one of the cosmic principalities and powers can withdraw himself from the transformation that takes place on that day.[9] How could Jesus Christ be fully revealed as *Lord* over all were he not Lord of all lords and did he not prove himself such? As early as the resurrection, Christ was given full power over all powers, but there was still space and time for them to be subordinated to him in successive acts of submission. The overcoming of death was reserved for the final triumph. The Last Day, however, signifies an end of all that might be called development or

6 Is. 40:5; Luke 3:6; 1 Cor. 13:12; 1 John 3:2; Rev. 1:7. In the intervening time, already, the confession of faith was determined by the reciprocity of the process of knowing. At that time, however, human knowledge stood in an unequal relation to the anticipatory, universally penetrating knowledge of God, who "knows all things." Cf. 1 John 3:20; Gal. 4:9; 1 Cor. 2:9ff.; 8:2-3; Matt. 11:27; John 10:14-15.

7 Rev. 5:5-14.

8 1 Thess. 5:2; 2 Thess. 2:2; 1 Cor. 1:8; 2 Cor. 1:14; Phil. 1:6, 19; 2:16.

9 2 Thess. 1—2; Matt. 24:15-31, etc.

process. On this day all powers including death are conquered and subjugated.[10] Such promises cannot be explained. They can only be repeated and accepted in faith and hope, for no theology, no drama, no vision can suggest what is meant by saying that God will be "all in all."

Only this much can be said: precisely those powers that had led men into temptation, that had falsely been honored as divinities, that had wished to intervene between God and man as accusers of men and to barricade God's love,[11] now bow down before Christ. They are not simply annihilated;[12] they are brought with finality into that order which corresponds to their place in God's good creation. The Last Day discloses that in his judgment of Jews and Gentiles God was thinking of his whole creation and took mercy on all his works. As Christ's death meant a co-crucifixion not only of men but also of the world,[13] so his glorification is a confirmation of the world—and more than this, it is the new creation of heaven and earth. The "new man" whom God had made had always been an earnest and a presaging of a new creation.[14] Now in the Last Judgment, the conclusive subordination of all powers proves that God's judging is in the end edification, building up; that in setting things *right* he has set them *upright* and saved his whole creation. [15] As early as in the second Isaiah,[16] the creation of the world, the saving of the people and the nations, and the manifestation of God's

[10] Phil. 2:10-11; Rom. 14:11; 1 Cor. 15:25-28; cf. Matt. 28:18.

[11] 1 Thess. 3:5; Gal. 4:8; 1 Cor. 7:5; 8:5; Rom. 1:23; 8:31-39; Col. 2:18-23.

[12] See M. E. Dahl, "The Resurrection of the Body," *Studies in Biblical Theology*, XXXVI (1962), esp. 117-119, for a discussion of the Greek verb meaning "make of no effect, cancel."

[13] Gal. 6:14. Especially in 2 Thess.; 2 Pet. 3; Matt. 24 and parallels; and in Rev., the passion and death of Jesus Christ are mirrored not only in the persecution of the church and the death of martyrs but also in the catastrophe that befalls all nature. All creation "has been groaning together until now" under the corruption and decay that oppress it (Rom. 8:19-22). This is not an accident, nor fate, nor the consequence of some inherent corruption, but the outcome of God's Judgment.

[14] Besides Rom. 8:19ff., see also Gal. 6:15; 1 Cor. 4:6; 2 Cor. 5:17; Eph. 2:10, 16; Jas. 1:18.

[15] In German, *Richten* can mean *Aufrichten*.

[16] With special clarity in 51:4-6, 9-16.

righteousness were seen and proclaimed as a unity. The essence of God's justifying Judgment would be denied not only by a final separation of the doctrine of creation from the doctrine of salvation but also by an anthropological narrowing or a theology that ignores or belittles the world.

3. Man himself will be revealed and glorified

Since the Last Judgment brings the validation of God as Creator and Savior of the whole world, it is impossible that man will be left out in the cold. "When Christ, our life, appears, then we also will appear with him in glory." "We are now children of God, and it is not yet made manifest what we shall be. But we know that when he appears, we will be like him." "We, gazing with uncovered faces at the glory of the Lord, will be changed into the same image, from glory to glory." "On that day God will judge the hidden things of men, according to my Gospel, through Jesus Christ." "The Lord will come, who will light up the darkness." "The inward Jew will receive his praise not from men, but from God."[17] Just as the rising sun lights up every object that is touched by its rays, the revelation of Jesus Christ the Judge means that all men are now drawn into the light and presented glorious.

The Last Day therefore brings not only the unveiling of something exalted that was previously hidden *from* men but also the unveiling of something concealed *in* men. As the Judge manifests his righteousness, the rightness or wrongness of man also comes to light. If there is anything at all in or about them which is right, their righteousness will be like his. Since Christ was not only installed as their virtual or potential representative but actually as the fully empowered manager of their case, now that Jesus Christ is judging them their case cannot possibly be lost altogether.

What, however, is the hidden thing that now comes to light? It cannot possibly be a righteousness of their own, which was inherent in them before the Judgment or infused after some phase of it. Such a righteousness was always out of the question; all men were found

17 Col. 3:4; 1 John 3:2; 2 Cor. 3:18; 1 Cor. 15:49; Rom. 2:16, 29; 1 Cor. 4:5.

indeed to be sinners and only by the life and the Spirit, which were newly given by God, were they fitted for thanksgiving, love, community, and confession.[18] Neither can this revelation have to do with the glorification of "works of the law," single or accumulated, that were done before Good Friday, or the glorification of especially noble deeds and sacrifices that were completed after Easter. For even when a man fancies that he is living "blamelessly according to the righteousness of the law" or living as a Christian with an unblemished conscience, in the sight of God he can only say, "I consider that to be filthy excrement"; "I am not justified even by that."[19] Lastly it is not a matter of praising human passivity. A man can rebel against God just as strongly in laziness, cowardice, and passivity as in calculation or open revolution.

What becomes open to view on the Last Day, rather, is the whole man who has actively done many things and passively let many things go by him. The essence of this man is nothing other than his *existence* in doing these things, in suffering those things and in omitting or resisting other things.[20] Knowingly or unknowingly, willingly or unwillingly, externally driven or internally motivated, he

[18] Gal. 2:15, 17, 20; 3:2ff.; Rom. 3:10-20, 22-23; 5:12; 6–8; Eph. 2:1-10.
[19] Phil. 3:6-8; 1 Cor. 4:2-5.
[20] Man—in Paul, as in existentialist thought—is identical with his history. He is what he does and what he experiences, and not an abstract "substance" to which actions and experiences are tacked on as "accidents." Were God not gracious to him who has his own special history, to the man who is identical with his actions and experiences, he would not be dealing with the real man at all. Cf. the passages cited in note 3 above (pp. 74-75) and E. Jüngel's remarks on this theme. God is not judging a bare framework or a *tabula rasa*. There is no looking on men as nameless cattle, no assigning them to be turned out to this or that pasture; but, as with a father dealing with his children, there are personal communion and communication at the Last Judgment between God and man. As a man is presented before God's Judgment, he is laid bare and judged with his deeds. He is not stripped of his body, i.e., of his bodily life and of his bodily deeds and omissions, in order to stand naked; rather the mortal and corruptible is "clothed over" (2 Cor. 5:1-10; 1 Cor. 15:53-54). It is probable that the resurrection of the body, which is proclaimed especially in 1 Cor. 15:35-54, has less to do with the physical meaning of "body" than with an understanding of "body" that comprehends the whole man. "Whole man" here means not only—indeed not primarily—a man's relation to himself (as R. Bultmann tried to make credible in his interpretation of "body" in *Theology of the New Testament*, I, 195ff.), but rather man in his relation to God, who has given him body and soul, and in his dealing with his fellow men and with his environment of things and events.

has proven unfaithful toward God and loveless in relation to his neighbors. But, at the urging of the Spirit, beginnings have been made in praying to God, praising him, loving brothers, selflessly serving persons far and near, living in peace. Whether a man must now accuse himself of not achieving the good he had intended to perform, or whether he looks back with reasonable certainty on a completion of the good fight and is not aware of making any missteps,[21] before God's judgment neither the man nor his fellows know what all his deeds, sufferings, and omissions amount to.

Indeed, "what is good, acceptable to God and perfect," man has been enabled to "examine, . . . search out, test [or, find out by experience]."[22] The law was a "useful" signpost for him in this; the Scripture has given him good exhortations; mutual brotherly assistance and counsel were not in vain[23] —although all this could be misused and often was. But nothing is good or bad in itself. A thing is good only when God looks on it as good and just, and when he accepts it as such. He who alone is good is the only one to determine what is good. Nothing *has* to please God, but it is God's good pleasure to hear many a prayer; and he looks with pleasure on the service and suffering of his saints. Nothing is perfected, nothing is perfect in itself. But when a man is conformed to the image of Christ, he may stand faultless, holy, and perfect in the light of the "type" and representation of true manhood, Jesus Christ. The Last

Calvin (*Inst.* III. xvii. 3-4; cf. W. Niesel, *The Theology of Calvin*, tr. H. Knight [Philadelphia: Westminster Press, 1956], pp. 135ff.) held that a man's person is accepted in the justification effected by the cross and Easter, and that the Last Judgment supplements this first justification with a second in which, by grace alone, the works of the justified persons are accepted by God. Thus he differentiated a justification of the person from a justification of his works. This division, however, appears artificial if not arbitrary. The opinion of H. Schlier (*Der Brief an die Epheser*, 2d ed. [Düsseldorf: Patmos Verlag, 1958], p. 116), according to which "man is more than his works" and the works are only "the demonstrations of his existence," is equally difficult to document biblically.

21 See, for example, Rom. 7:18; 2 Tim. 4:7-8; 1 Cor. 4:3-4; 13:1-3; Acts 20:26-27; cf. 1 Sam. 12:3-5; Matt. 25:31-46, etc.

22 Rom. 12:2; Phil. 4:8; Eph. 5:10, etc.

23 The usefulness of the law is described by, e.g., Rom. 13:8-10; Luke 10:25-28; 1 Tim. 1:8; the right use of the Scriptures by, e.g., Rom. 15:4; 2 Tim. 3:16; Luke 16:29; and the place of brotherly exhortation by, e.g., 1 Thess. 4:18; 5:11; 2 Cor. 1:4; Rom. 1:12; 12:1.

Judgment reveals that true sonship, obedience, and love which, in eternity and in time, were included "in Christ" as man's share.

Therefore the final Judgment Day has an eminently anthropological significance. It reveals that the doing and suffering of men, their seeking and casting about, their venturing and their finding are worth something and are a long way from deserving Job's and Qoheleth's summary condemnation: "in vain." On the contrary, this Judgment makes it manifest that God intends to take pleasure in the action and the suffering of men. In accordance with the gracious verdict which Jesus Christ will pronounce in the name of God, it is "not in vain"—let alone a curse or humiliation—to be a man. The works of God will justify the Creator. To his works belongs—*man*. Therefore even the works of God's final and favorite creature, man, will on that day justify God. God's right will not triumph at the expense of man's right; rather it will triumph as God gives man his right and man is allowed to praise God's righteousness.

In order to give man the hope of this, God has appointed no one else but his Son, the advocate of men, to carry out the Judgment. Because Jesus Christ will appear as the Judge, men may look forward to the Last Day with their heads up.[24] God is well pleased with his Son; this pleasure overflows upon those whom his Son represents.

All works and all men must, indeed, go through the fire of the verdict of Jesus Christ.[25] This Judge certainly will so judge that hidden things come to light. Men who did not know when and how they really had accepted and honored Christ will now discover to their amazement that Christ knew them well and accepted their service. The "good works" for which men have been made anew by God are distinguished from "works of the law" by a humbling criterion: no man can or will boast about them.[26] They are not done out of any calculating ulterior motive that looks to a reward but because, in the right moment, a man can do no other; he *must* do the right thing and allow the "fruit of the Spirit" to ripen. While much thought and effort may indeed stand behind many great works

[24] Cf. Luke 21:28: "Lift up your heads!"; the Heidelberg Catechism, Question 52, refers to this passage in describing the Last Judgment.

[25] 1 Cor. 3:12-15; 2 Cor. 10:18; Rom. 2:28-29.

[26] Eph. 2:9-10; Matt. 25:34-40; Gal. 5:22-23.

of men, the Last Judgment will show that, for the really good works, the doers had no idea that they were doing anything good. There is grace only in a noble deed unconsciously done, not in self-conscious do-gooding. Every man is made aware in the Last Judgment of works, hitherto hidden from himself and others. Those works will be pronounced just. Otherwise, how could any man think of the Last Judgment with anything other than a shudder?

The Last Judgment is the guarantee that "in the Lord your labor is not in vain."[27] God justifies his work of creation and salvation to the embarrassment of all who had disbelieved in theodicy. He justifies himself by showing that he is pleased with the man he has created anew. Resurrection, glorification, clothing over, renewal, changing a fleshly into a spiritual body—all these are designations for one and the same event: the public, glorious, incontestable, and irrevocable justification of man through God's grace.

There is a shadow side of the judgment, however, that corresponds to the beams of light. No man will be justified except on the ground of Jesus Christ's prayer for sinners, God's hearing of the prayer, and the Spirit's renewing work. The man who prefers his own or his fellow's judgment to God's must be a fool, a man with a death-wish, a harvester of nothing but corruption. The Last Judgment will show that only God is right in his judgment and that his grace is the only power on which his creatures can rely. There is no salvation apart from God or in opposition to him; the only alternative to God's saving righteousness is horror and agony. Still, the justifying Judgment of God calls all men to faith. In time and eternity, this Judgment will be replaced by no other. The creatures can rely on the Creator.

27 With *these* words Paul closes the resurrection chapter, 1 Cor. 15.

Index of Proper Names

Index of Biblical Passages

INDEX OF BIBLICAL PASSAGES